T0158931

After a *Meal* Like This, You Don't Need *Dessert!*

A Menu of Times Gone By

Jack Connery

authorHOUSE®

AuthorHouse™
1663 Liberty Drive
Bloomington, IN 47403
www.authorhouse.com
Phone: 1 (800) 839-8640

Published by AuthorHouse 09/20/2017

ISBN: 978-1-5462-0767-2 (sc)
ISBN: 978-1-5462-0765-8 (hc)
ISBN: 978-1-5462-0766-5 (e)

Library of Congress Control Number: 2017913832

Print information available on the last page.

Any people depicted in stock imagery provided by Thinkstock are models, and such images are being used for illustrative purposes only.
Certain stock imagery © Thinkstock.

This book is printed on acid-free paper.

Contents

Title	Year	Page
The Setting	1934-1956	1
The Night I Saw Santa	1939	11
Hangin' On A Nail	1940	15
A Friend Made - - A Friend Lost	1940	19
I Went To School	1940	27
The War	1941-45	31
A Gift For Suzanne	1942	37
OurReligion	1935-55	39
Tastes Great? Less Filling?	1943	45
My Relationship With Dad	1943-50	49
The Front Yard	1943-50	55
Delivering Papers	1944-51	59
Just Sew Him Up, Doc!	1944	63
A Letter To Joe	1944	65
Bathroom Doors	1940-50	69
Home Entertainment	1940-50	71
An Unscheduled Afternoon At Bob's	1944	75
A Week In Tulsa	1944-48	77
Fourth Of July	1940-50	81
Going To The Dentist	1944-50	85
Milk Cream And Butter	1944-48	87
Watermelon		89
Headed To Camp	1946	91
John Rodgers' Farm	1946-48	97
Ruben Utley	1946-47	99
Counting Sheep	1946	101
Gene Flowers	1942-50	103
All-Night Parties	1946-50	105
Bob Finkel Arrives	1947	107
Ordering Groceries	1935-50	109
What's A Patio?	1947	113
Presbyterian Youth Group	1947-45	117
The Ol' Swimmin' Hole	1947-52	119

My Show Calf	1947	121
Mutt And Keith	1947-51	123
Saturday Night In The Projection Room	1948	127
The Gift Of Life	1948-53	131
Sundays In Tulsa	1948-53	133
We Make New Friends	1948	135
To The Showers	1949	137
What Ever Happened To Pep Clubs?	1949-51	139
Buck	1949	141
Hunting	1946-52	145
Booster Trips	1949-52	149
The Day Dad Died	1949-50	153
Off To War Again	1950-51	157
Draggin' Main	1950-52	161
The World Of Work	1943-56	165
The Club	1950-53	171
Fundraising	1950-53	175
Rudy	1950-52	179
Television In Broken Arrow	1951	183
Shelby - - What Is Education?	1951	187
The Junior-Senior Fight	1951	189
Growing Up Too Early	1951	195
Matootin's Tooters	1951-52	201
Braces Unnecessary	1951-52	205
Who Wants Panties?	1952	207
My Love Life	1949-56	209
Dropping OU Band	1952	213
Luck Runs Out	1952	215
Tom And Pat's Wedding	1955	219
I Met Mary Kathryn	1955	223
My Senior Year	1956	227
The Day I Became Jack	1956	233
So You Want To Be An Officer?	1945-58	235
Influences		239

Foreword

My parents were already deceased when my last uncle passed away and I realized that there was no one left who could tell me about the early life of my parents, and things that I wanted to know. I decided that my children, and their children would not experience this. So, I have written the story of my early life. It is the story of a young boy, growing up in a farm family in a small Oklahoma town during dust bowl days, the Great Depression and World War II.

It is a story about growing up without T-ball, little league, television, X-box, laptops and cell phones. It is the story about living in the same house throughout one's childhood. It is the story of graduating from high school with the same kids you started first grade. It is the story about going off to the University of Oklahoma, 120 miles away and the farthest from home I had ever been. It is a story about leaving Oklahoma for the first time as a junior in college. After passing this draft to my children, I asked them to compare it with their lives, where they lived in 15 houses, in 10 cities on both the East and West Coasts, in six states and a U.S. possession overseas during my career as a naval officer. They went to school in eight school systems. They were almost nomadic, never having the time to develop a close friendship. I saw Tulsa County and they saw the nation.

This is a book of stories about incidents in my life. Except for personalities that carry over, each is independent of the others. One can pick up at any point one desires although it is recommended that the Setting be read first.

Writing this book has given me a chance to relive my childhood.

I have relived good times and bad times; happy times and sad times. I have laughed and I have cried. I have felt the disappointment in failure, and the elation in success. In retrospect, my childhood was excellent and I would be happy to live it again.

I would recommend that anyone in their senior years undertake this task. It will make you young again, and be a blessing to your offspring.

Acknowledgements

Without the help of many, this project would not have been completed, and I sincerely offer them my thanks.

To my family, my late parents and my late brothers and sister, for creating the environment that made this story possible. I have tried to be accurate. If there are distortions, omissions, or exaggerations, I apologize.

To my daughters and son, for providing a reason to tell it.

To my highschool classmates, who helped me years ago sort out information

To my good friends, who thought this project was such a good idea and continually encouraged me to complete it.

To my wife Jill, for persevering with me and for her editing skills

And to Susan Shinn Turner, editor and friend, for her final edit.

This book is dedicated to my daughters Kathleen, Margaret, Susan, and Patricia; and my son Michael. I suggest that as you age, you do this same thing

The Setting

It was about 2 a.m., Monday, June 4, 1934, when my life began at St. John's Hospital, Tulsa, Oklahoma. My birth certificate describes me as having green eyes, being 20 inches long, and weighing 7 1/2 pounds. I was a "well baby," delivered by Dr. Carl Simpson, and the fourth son of Michael Joseph and Annabelle Dorothy (Eustice) Connery.

It was customary to keep a new mother and child in the hospital for 8-10 days. After about a week, Dad brought us home to Broken Arrow, where we were greeted by my brothers Tom, 4, Bill, 7, and Horace, (Mike) 9. Home was Arrow Farm, 3/4 mile east of downtown Broken Arrow, Oklahoma, a small farm community of less than 3,000 population, located in what is now called Green Country, in the northeastern part of Oklahoma.

Those were tough times, just 5 years after the complete collapse of the stock market and the beginning of the Great Depression. The country's economy had gone downhill since that time, and recovery had not yet begun. Two years before my birth, the Democratic Party had won the White House with Franklin Delano Roosevelt, and the promise that "Happy Days are Here Again."

On top of that, western Oklahoma had become a dust bowl, shutting down thousands of acres of farm land. Many families were driven westward toward California in rickety old vehicles containing all of their possessions. They were enticed by advertisements for farm laborers and the hope of jobs and better times. The term Okies was born. Eastern Oklahoma was spared from the dust bowl, but we could look westward and see the dust clouds in the sunset.

Thousands and thousands were unemployed. Many, who had earlier achieved various degrees of success, were standing in soup lines. Although we never had to do that, we were poor by today's standards. We just did not know it. Mom always put good food on the table, and we never left the table hungry. Poor seemed to be a way of life and for most people in town, and that kind of equality continued through high school. Someone once defined "poor" as a "state of mind," and "broke" as a "temporary condition." If these definitions are reasonably accurate, we were never poor, but we were broke most of the time.

Home was a 20-acre farm. Arrow Farm was primarily a poultry operation, consisting of three long chicken houses, one long brooder house and four smaller chicken houses. A huge hay barn was a geographical reference point, sitting across the dirt Lynn Lane Road from the high school football field. Additionally, there was a barn for half a dozen milk cows and a pig run.

In the late 1920's, Dad had a milk, egg and vegetable route, selling the products he raised. He named the place Arrow Farms and proudly painted this logo on the side of a Model T Ford farm truck.

The house was small, sitting in the middle of a clump of elm trees, 300 feet from the road. When I was born, there were two bedrooms, with the plumbing outside. I don't know how my parents and brothers all fit, but they did. At my birth, construction started on two more bedrooms and plumbing came inside.

In addition to farming, Dad worked part-time as a foreman for the Soil Conservation Service. This was a program established throughout Oklahoma to provide land conservation services to cities, towns and rural areas. It was a fallout from the dust bowl days to get Oklahoma's land back in shape, and preserve it. When the Civilian Conservation Corps established a camp across the road in 1935, Dad went to work with them as a foreman, after completing an orientation course at Oklahoma A&M College, 60 miles away. The CCC was a para-military program established by President Roosevelt to provide jobs and to help get the country back on its feet from the depression. The camp had over 15 buildings and 200 young men. Dad supervised a number of men on various conservation projects. He had a high school education, and two years of vocational training. Mom was a mother and housewife. She had not much more than an eighth grade education.

We farmed. At first, it was just chickens, but Arrow Farms grew to include beef, pigs, dairy cows and finally, sheep. In addition, we grew our own vegetables on a 5-acre tract, as well as those included in Dad's produce route. Most of our bread was home baked. Spring and summer were gardening time, which was always followed by canning. We butchered pork and beef in the fall, and either canned or cured it. It was common to kill a chicken on Saturday for Sunday dinner. There was no such thing as a deep freeze. Years later, we were able to rent a freezer locker at a downtown grocery store.

One of my earliest memories was running out through the front yard to meet Dad as he came home from work. He would drop his lunch pail and place me, his little "curly top," on his shoulders and walk back to the house.

The town only extended three blocks east and west of Main Street, so we were in the country, even though across the road from the city limits. I remember when we first got a telephone, the address listed in the directory was "east of city." We weren't far enough out to have a route number, but were too far out to be a part of town. The telephone system was so small, our phone number was only three digits, and we were on a party line with our neighbor. Only one of us could use the phone at a time. It was frustrating to need to use the phone and find that the neighbor had left the phone off the hook. As the town got larger, the number was increased to four digits, 4821. That number remained until Mom sold the place in 1955. There was no mail delivery, so we had Box 503 at the post office downtown. We were far enough out that we weren't included in city delivery, and not far enough to be on a rural route.

On August 1, 1936, one of the hottest summers on record, we were blessed with a baby sister, Mary Margaret. Being the only girl in a family with four older brothers had to be difficult for her, but Mary was always able to hold her own. Dad was extremely proud to finally have a daughter after all those boys.

A year later, Dad got sick. He had been going downhill for 3-4 months, caused by periods of extreme coughing. Breathing had been a problem for him since his WWI stint as a foot soldier and his exposure to a number of German mustard gas attacks in France and Germany. Now, he contracted tuberculosis. Medical thinking at the time was that the gas attacks had weakened his lungs, permitting his illness. There wasn't much of a cure for TB then. Many thought that dryer climates would help. The medical procedure, at least in Dad's case, was to cut it out. He was sent to the VA hospital in Chicago where doctors removed one lung and about half of the other, and as many ribs across the back as necessary to get to the lungs. Here was a young man, in his early 40s, crippled for the rest of his life. How far medical science has come! Today, it is prevented with a shot and treated with a pill. For the next few years, he was in and out of two VA hospitals in Oklahoma and the one in Chicago, 300 miles away. The extensive rehabilitation kept him away from home for most of the next three years. He would never be able to work regularly again. Since we had all been exposed to TB, we had to have tests and x-rays annually for many years afterwards.

That changed our whole way of life. As we kids became old enough, we picked up our share of the load. Mom, with just her limited education, had to become the breadwinner. In those late depression years, there weren't many jobs available for a woman, especially for one who had little education. However, her work experience at Gypsy Oil before her marriage, gave her an edge. During those years President Roosevelt instituted many programs to get the country back on its feet, such as the CCC camps mentioned earlier, the National Recovery Act and Works Progress Administration, etc. Mom got a job with the WPA as a clerk. These kinds of programs built high school gyms, National Guard armories, and highways across the country.

My older brother tells me that we were qualified to go to one of these agencies and get clothes. They were a standard issue--almost a uniform type of dress. We never did. Mom was just too proud. We wore bib overalls and knickers a lot. As the youngest, my wardrobe mainly consisted of hand-me-downs. We always went to school neat and clean, although with occasional patches on the knees and elbows. In later years, patches on the elbows of sports jackets were the fashion. And now, jeans with holes in the knees and shredded legs sell for the highest dollar. It makes me proud to know we were the forerunners of fashion.

When Mom went to work, she needed help in the home, if for no other reason, to keep law and order among us kids. Ruby, a Creek Indian lady, filled that role for a few years.

In 1940, I started school. Hitler and his German armies marched across Europe that year. A year later, the Japs bombed Pearl Harbor, and we were at war. Like many other young men, Mike and Bill wanted to quit school and join the service. Cousins Don Eustice and Hank Southwood, both older, had finished high school and were already gone. Dad would not permit it. Realizing the importance of a high school education, he insisted that they finish. As soon as they graduated, they enlisted in the Navy.

When Mike was close to graduation, Dad counseled him on a choice of service. Dad had been a foot soldier in a messy war, and spent a lot of time in trenches and foxholes. "I don't think you want to be a foot soldier," he said. "I don't know much about life on a ship, but I heard that sailors, even in wartime, have three hot meals a day, get a shower once a week, and sleep between clean sheets at night." That obviously was what convinced Mike to join the Navy. It set a trend, as Bill, Tom, and I followed in his footsteps and went to sea on ships when our time came.

After the war started, Douglas Aircraft built a bomber plant in northeast Tulsa. Mom went to work in there, 20 miles away. She wasn't a "Rosie the Riveter," as depicted on wartime posters, but was close. She rode a work bus most of those years. We had no car, and she didn't drive anyway. She rotated occasionally to the evening shift (3:30 to midnight), and when I was old enough, I would meet her at the bus stop, on the other side of the old CCC camp, after midnight and walk home with her. She was in a job where she was always on her feet on concrete all through the work day. This caused problems with her feet, and I remember the many nights she rolled her feet on a tennis ball or baseball to strengthen her arches. As kids, we did a lot of things to support the war effort. Those efforts are described later.

Meanwhile, Dad got back into as much good health as he would ever get, and he became the chief cook and bottle washer at home. His tools were an iron skillet, a few pots and pans and a spatula. His specialty was Spanish rice. He became an excellent baker of fresh rolls and bread. Every other day, Mary and I would come home from school in the afternoon to the aroma of fresh baked bread coming from the kitchen. Dad would take the little scraps of dough left over and make miniature loaves for an afternoon snack. Splitting one of those down the middle when it was still hot, filling it with home-made butter, closing it up and eating it with a glass of milk, I was in hog heaven. Occasionally, he would roll any excessive dough out, sprinkle sugar and cinnamon on it and bake it 'til crisp. What a delight these were. His cinnamon rolls were fantastic. Dad became an excellent cook. There was always plenty of excellent food to eat. We never left the table hungry. There were times when we might have been short on potatoes, meat or another item, but there were always other items to fill in, such as another slice of bread and butter.

Eating was always better in the summer. There was always fresh peas, green beans, corn, squash and potatoes. We had at least one fresh vegetable daily.

Dad would often back away from the table and say, "After a good meal like that, we don't need dessert." That's because we didn't have dessert. That's the way it was. We rarely had dessert during the week. On Sunday things were different. Mom might bake a cake or a pie, and sometimes, we had homemade ice cream to go with it. Dad learned to make bread pudding, which became his favorite dessert.

With the help of those there and able, Dad also maintained the farm. He always maintained a good workshop with sufficient tools to make any repairs necessary. Dad was always thin. His hands and arms were nothing but skin and bones, and always seemed delicate. He couldn't do anything without bleeding.

We were raised Catholic. Dad and Mom were very devout people. In the mid 1930s, my family carved out two acres of road frontage property on the south side of the farm, and donated it to the church. A little stone church was torn down in Jenks, about 10 miles away, was moved stone by stone to the property, and reassembled. We had a church. Father Joseph Griffin was assigned to St. Anne's and a small rectory was moved in. In the early days, as the church was being built, Sunday services, always with just a few attendees, were held in our front yard.

We went to Mass every Sunday and all Holy Days, and at least Mom went every day during Lent. I went to catechism classes on Saturday and learned about my religion. I had begun learning the Latin prayers of the Mass and what they meant. I was on the way to becoming an altar boy. Father Griffin became an army chaplain after the war started. We went throughout the war without a priest, going to church only when a "circuit rider" came to town, or on special occasions, when an uncle would drive out from Tulsa and take us back to Sunday mass.

As we grew up, entertainment, for the most part, was what we made of it. We made a lot of our own toys. We'd often cut up an old tire tube, cut out a gun from 1x4 pine and make rubber guns. With clothes pins and notches along the barrel, we could make what we called machine guns. We made scooters and wagons out of old lumber and ball bearing wheels. We played in barns, around the pond, and climbed trees. We rode Daisy, a Shetland pony. Later, Mary had her own big horse named Pete. At night, we would gather around the radio and listen to the likes of Fibber McGee and Molly, Inner Sanctum and Jack Benny.

Saturday was the big day. For a quarter, we could go to the movie and sit through it as many times as we wanted. With the change, we could buy a box of popcorn and a coke for a nickel each, and still have a nickel left over to start the next week. We would also see an episode of a Superman, Dick Tracy, or similar serial, which kept us coming back every week. And we saw the Movietone News, where we learned what was happening in the world, especially about the war.

All of us boys, when we got old enough, had Tulsa Tribune or Tulsa World paper routes. I started about age 9 or 10. It was a way to earn and save money. Mom would take part of the money and invest in savings stamps and bonds. These would be held in secure places and would be mighty helpful when college time came. Paper routes eventually got me a scholarship, which helped in starting college. When I was a teenager, we had the whole town, morning and evening. Mom supervised. I delivered two routes, and we hired boys to deliver the others.

We had a stable school system with regard to teachers as well as students. Twenty of the kids I started first grade with graduated with me 12 years later. The lady who taught Mike in the second grade taught the rest of us in the second grade, and was still teaching when Mary graduated. My high school principal became superintendent 15 years later and my high school assistant football coach eventually became coach then high school principal. Like any school, we had some fantastic teachers, and we had some poor ones. With the former, we were guided and encouraged in our education. With the latter, it was all up to us--we had to scratch for everything we got. Unfortunately, I was never highly motivated to do much scratching without guidance. The teachers who were non-motivating were also the ones who were easily manipulated by the students. So, there was a tradeoff. We had fun, even if we didn't learn much.

One day the war was over, and Mike and Bill came home. To this day, I remember going to the train station to help welcome Mike and other veterans. Servicemen were discharged on a point system, and we checked regularly to see how many points they had. We had gone to the station several days expecting to see Mike, to no avail. Finally, it was so good to have them home. Many came home wounded. Others, like my cousin Pat, did not come home. Using the GI Bill, both of my older brothers went to Tulsa University. After schooling at TU, Purdue University and Oklahoma A&M, Mike finished with a master's degree in psychology. Bill quit college after his third year. In 1948 Tom finished high school and went to Oklahoma A&M, now Oklahoma State. He got his degree in 1952, the year I began college.

After the war, when Douglas phased down, Mom went to work for the U.S. Corps of Engineers in downtown Tulsa. Again, she had to carpool. She worked there through the day she died in 1969, two years short of retirement.

My Dad got sick again in December 1949, took a turn for the worse in January and died at the Veterans' hospital in Muscogee.

In 1950, the North Koreans crossed the Yalu River into South

Korea and our country was involved in a "police action." Bill and Mike, who were still in the Naval Reserve, were recalled to active duty. Because of Mike's education and the degree he had just received, he was commissioned as a clinical psychologist in the Medical Service Corps, and remained in the Navy for a career, retiring as a captain. When Tom graduated from A&M, he was commissioned in the Navy, and caught the tail end of the Korean War. Bill served one year then was released on a hardship discharge because he was married and had two children.

During my sophomore year, I discovered girls and began dating. Over the next two years, I dated a number of girls, had crushes on some of them, but never really had a "steady" in high school.

There were a lot of influences on me during these next few years, some good and some not so good. In spite of various problems I got myself into, I think the good influences far out-numbered the others. It was almost a given in my mind that I would go to college, but really had no idea what I wanted to study. At the start of my senior year, I decided I wanted to be a writer, and everything after that was directed toward that goal. At an earlier time, I thought I would like to be a dentist, but I realized that my science background wasn't good enough. When I learned I would lose my front teeth as a result of a previous football injury, I lost that desire for dentistry.

So, after graduation and working that summer, off to the University of Oklahoma I went, 120 miles away, the farthest I had been from home, to learn to be a famous sports writer. Bob Considine and Grantland Rice had become my sports writing idols. I struggled through OU, having all sorts of problems with the likes of Latin, geology, botany and math. I really enjoyed the history, English and journalism courses. I graduated in June 1956. I had met Mary Kathryn Mideke the previous fall, and we were married June 2, 1956, the day before graduation.

In 1955, Mom sold the farm, and bought a home in Tulsa, not far from her brother and sister. Mary was the last one at home (She had graduated from high school in 1954) and the place was just too big for them to take care of. In later years, an apartment house and a convenience store were built in the front yard with our old house and barn going to ruin behind.

The draft into military service was still in effect, and I had been told I would be called immediately after graduation. Local draft boards still had quotas to meet. I remembered Dad's advice to Mike about choice of services. That spring, knowing that I would have a degree, I applied for Navy Officer Candidate School, and eventually was accepted. Before going, however, I worked the summer as a news reporter for the Oklahoma City Times.

When I left for the Navy in August 1956, the Times gave me a leave of absence, because I would be back in three years. However, saltwater got in my blood, and that resulted in a 21-year career in the Navy. When I served aboard a ship in Charleston, South Carolina, some years later, my neighbor was the sports Editor for the local paper. He used to comment that I left one poor paying profession for another.

The Night I Saw Santa

"**S**anta does exist! I know. I saw him!" Those were the words I used that Christmas morning. Until that time, I had heard enough skepticism that I had some doubts. "He had on a red suit, had a big white beard and was fat, and he carried a big bag of toys over his shoulder," I exclaimed to Mom, Dad and my brothers over and over. Now, I knew, and I was excited about that. There were presents under the tree to prove to those who didn't believe me.

I must have been 5 years old that Christmas Eve when I went to bed. We had walked to midnight mass at the little Catholic church next door. We visited the Baby Jesus in the crib and ended the service with the singing of "Silent Night" which put all of us in a Christmas spirit. The walk home into that freezing north wind, now blowing snowflakes, set the weather for the night. I wondered if Santa would really come. The cold wind and blowing snow encountered on that short walk home was enough for me. I wondered how he would survive it on his trip around the world. The skeptics had not gotten to my sister Mary so she was really excited, hoping he would bring that doll with the golden hair she had seen in the Sears catalog.

The awkward-looking limb, cut from the cedar tree in front of the house, served as a Christmas tree, and leaned into a corner of the living room, held up by the two walls where they came together. The lights, tinsel, popcorn strung together by needle and thread, and colored balls weighed heavily on the limb's branches. Dad and Mike had cut the limb two days ago. The cedar was a beautiful tree, not all that tall, but broad and full. It provided a lot of shade from the western sun on hot summer days, but it also stood in the shade of massive elm and maple trees.

We could have bought one in town at Lloyd's Grocery, but the few available were expensive. A few would have been stacked in a back corner of the store. There was no such thing as a Christmas tree lot in Broken Arrow. We could have gone to the country and cut one, probably along the coal pits where we swam as kids. But we didn't do that either.

At the right time, about three days before Christmas, Dad would pick the limb to cut. Mike or Bill, and in later years Tom or I, would scale the tree, saw in hand, and cut out the selected limb. We would bring it in the house, prop it up in a bucket of sand so that it was as straight as possible, perhaps trim it somewhat. Years later, I went back to the old homestead (I've been back several times since retiring from the Navy and returning to Oklahoma). One thing I did look at closely this time was that old cedar tree. It was still there, still somewhat flourishing, but not as healthy as it was years ago. It is sandwiched in closely between the front of the house and the apartment building sitting in our front yard. When I looked up into the tree, I could see many gaps--many places where in the past, Christmas tree limbs had been cut out. A stranger would wonder why the tree was ever trimmed like that.

After a cup of hot chocolate and a piece of Aunt Maggie's fruitcake, Mary and I were hurried off to bed after placing two big cookies and a glass of milk on the kitchen table for Santa. Not much later, Mike and Bill bundled up and rode their bikes off to deliver their morning paper routes. I was excited, as any kid my age would be on Christmas Eve. I had a hard time going to sleep. I woke in the middle of the night to Shep barking outside. I sensed that someone was in the room with me. I was startled, lying there in the dark trying to get my eyes adjusted. When I was finally able to see vague outlines of things, I saw him. I was frightened, and started to wake Tom, who was asleep next to me in the fold-out double bed. When I realized who it was I saw, I decided not to wake him.

The front door entry into our house came into our bedroom, one of two rooms added early in my life. In later chapters, when I talk about the house, I call this room the entry room, for lack of a better description, but for years, it was also Tom's and my bedroom.

We had no chimney for Santa to come down, so he had to enter through the front door. In spite of the darkness, once I saw his vague outline, he soon became clear, and his features were recognizable. We had a portable closet with an accordion type door just inside the front door. It was close to the foot of my bed. When I first saw him, he had the door open, and his whole upper torso was bent over, inside the closet. I knew there was nothing in there because that's where I kept my clothes. It was when he straightened, and backed out of the closet, that I recognized him. He turned toward me, saw that I was awake and sitting up in bed, and he gave me a big smile, and placed his index finger to his lips.

He was busy about the house, especially around the Christmas tree, for a few moments, then, with a wave of his hand, was gone out the front door. He said nothing. I want to say I heard sleigh bells, heard him shouting to his reindeer, but I didn't-- just the dog, continuing to bark. He was gone in an instant.

I got two toy trucks that Christmas. One was a dump truck, the other a wrecker. One was yellow, the other red. These were probably the only indestructible toys I ever had. It seems like I had them for years, and they were always my favorites. Mary got her Sears doll and smiled lovingly as she rocked it on her lap.

Later that day, we all gathered around the kitchen table for the traditional Christmas dinner—roasted turkey and dressing, mashed potatoes and giblet gravy, and green beans.

Every time I hear children talking, "Is there a Santa?" "Is he real?" I think about that. I think that perhaps there is a time when we all see him. I know I did. And he was real--perhaps only for young children. Because of that experience, however, he is still real for me.

Hangin' On A Nail

When all seven of us were home, every bed in the house was occupied at night. Most of us doubled up. Mike and Bill slept together in one room. Tom and I slept together in another. These two rooms and the bathroom were added to the house after I was born. I can't imagine the sleeping arrangements before these rooms were added. Mary shared a bedroom with Mom; Dad, because he was so frail and not well, slept alone in the back bedroom.

Things loosened up a little when Mike and Bill entered the service. Tom and I moved to their room, which left our bedroom as a front room.

It was very difficult to have someone over to spend the night. There was just no place for an extra to sleep. We had lots of cousins in Tulsa who would like to come to the farm for a week, and join in feeding the chickens and the cows, but there just wasn't room, unless it was summer and we slept outside - - in a tent, or just in the open. Mary would have slumber parties and all the girls slept outside. When I had a bunch over, we would usually go to the hay barn.

When we did have a guest over, Dad's favorite line, when it came to discussing sleeping arrangements, was, "I guess we'll have to hang you on a nail," he would say to a guest. We had a picture in the living room that hung on a big nail. Dad would describe how it would be done, using the straps of bib overalls to hang by. I don't remember how he would have hung up a girl. There were times when a guest would believe it, and became become reluctant to stay.

During those times, it was common for a drifter--perhaps that's not the right word, just a man down and out--to come by looking for a couple of hours of work in return for a hot meal and a place to sleep. The country was recovering from a major depression, but there were still many people homeless and unemployed. One afternoon a man came by that I really liked. He was clean and reasonably well dressed, and he talked well. He helped Dad set some fence posts at the dairy barn where we were building a new holding pen. He looked happy being useful. The smells, indicating a good meal, were already coming from the kitchen.

When the work was done and Dad and the man washed up at the outside well, he was permitted to join the family and eat with us at the table. Dad and Mom were always willing to share a meal with someone less fortunate. His name was Mr. Thompson and he was a banker by profession and had been unemployed the past three years. He had lost his home, and his wife and two children had gone back to Missouri to live with her parents. He told stories about wandering across country looking for work - - any kind of work that would end in a hot meal. He talked of friends who had committed suicide. Just barely 5 or 6, I listened in awe to his day by day adventures of living in the outdoors.

Finally, as Mom started clearing the table, I violated the old adage that "children should be seen, not heard," and asked the man if he would like to spend the night. "Now John," Mom scolded, "you know we don't have room." I kept pressing the issue, ending my argument by saying we could hang Dad on the nail. I even got up, and showed the man the nail. "Here," I said, "we can hang Dad here by the straps, and you can have his bed."

I could see that I was digging myself in deeper and deeper when I saw the frown on Dad's face. Fortunately, Mr. Thompson refused my invitation, but would accept an invitation to sleep in the barn. After dinner and a short conversation, he went to the barn and was gone the next morning. We all gathered in the living room and said a prayer for him and others like him. I hoped that some day, Mr. Thompson would come back. I got a stern lecture from Dad that night. "Don't you ever do anything like that again--ever," isn't too far from his remarks.

But this episode accomplished one thing. I don't remember Dad ever again talking about hanging someone on a nail.

When Mike and Bill were little, and the only two in the family, we had another visitor - - one who became part of the family for several years. Dad was summoned into town in 1929 and asked if he would take in a young boy traveling through the country looking for work, wherever he could find it. Jack Scissons was a young man from Saskatchewan, Canada. Dad agreed on condition that he would help on the farm and continue his education. Jack moved into the hay barn apartment and enrolled in Broken Arrow High School. He became a big brother to the younger boys, graduating in 1931. He then attended Oklahoma A&M College. After receiving his degree, he returned to Canada, where he became a pilot in the Royal Canadian Air Force and flew many combat missions over France and Germany during WWII. Jack never returned to Broken Arrow, but always maintained contact with his Broken Arrow family and friends. Twice, at two Christmases, he treated us with the beautiful Hudson Bay blankets with the big yellow, green and red stripes. One of them is still preserved in my possession.

A Friend Made - - A Friend Lost

I didn't have any friends - - people-friends, that is. Not that I didn't want any. There were just no other 6-year-old boys around. We were two miles out in the country. That's a long way when there is no transportation. That's why I enjoyed so much the times when folks like Mr. Thompson came by, looking for work. But those times were not the same as having a friend the same age. Listening to your brothers and parents all day was not the same either. We were chicken farmers, and in addition to the hundreds of chickens, there always seemed to be a dog, or a baby calf, or a pony, or perhaps a lamb. These were my friends.

At this point, I should mention my imaginary friend. I was so much in need of a friend that I created Arney Scroggins. Arney was about my age and size, and had bright red hair. I don't know where that name or the description came from, but it seemed to fit. He became my pal right off and he went everywhere I went. We became inseparable. One day Mom caught me talking to him and that kind of put him out of my life for awhile. I was afraid that my brothers, and my sister too, would tease and make fun of me if they knew about Arney.

"Arney, what are we gonna do today?" I would ask, as we tied our shoes in the morning. "Let's go to the barn and play in the loft," I would continue.

"Nah," would come the reply. "I want to play in the tree house." And so it went, until we decided on something.

I had a 4-year-old sister, Mary. Even without friends, I wondered why any boy would want to play with a younger sister. There were three older brothers, ranging in age from 10 to 16. For many of the same reasons, they did not want me around them.

It was a hot summer day of 1940, the afternoon sun smelled of drought, and the hot south wind would soon fill the air with dust. The small town of Broken Arrow was just beginning to recover from the depression. There was very little money and few jobs but since it was a farm community, there always seemed to be enough food to go around. My parents did not have a car, and Dad's truck had been disposed of the year before, so the only other means of transportation, none of which I had mastered, included a farm tractor, the older brother's rickety old bicycle, and Daisy, the Shetland pony.

When I wanted to go someplace I walked, or ran if in a hurry. That was not a problem, however, because there were few places to go. The most exciting thing in town was a Saturday or Sunday afternoon 10-cent movie, but I couldn't go there unless a brother was willing to take me. That was it. I wanted to reason with Mom that Arney and I could go, but I knew that wouldn't work. There was no organized T-ball or soccer, no Little League, no television, X-Box or computer games. Not even a McDonald's, Pizza Hut or Dairy Queen. The closest thing to a swimming pool was the farm pond, used for watering the livestock. There was also Brissey's pond to the north where the big boys often went. On an extremely hot day, one of my brothers might be talked into taking me for a swim. Dad and Mom forbade me to be in the pond by myself.

Dad had been sick for a long time, and was still away in a hospital. While Mom worked in an office in Broken Arrow, a Creek Indian lady named Ruby came to the house and watched after me and Mary. Older brothers Mike, Bill and Tom shared the necessary chores to keep the farm running. In addition to milking cows, the family always had a large garden and raised enough beef, pork, poultry and vegetable products to supply the family dinner table. Occasionally, there would be small chores, such as gathering eggs or pulling weeds in the garden, where I could help. That made me feel important and helped pass the time of day.

Aside from that, I was on my own. One day was like the one before and the next would be the same. I was up at the crack of dawn, dressed, my bed straightened, and had breakfast before Mom left for work. Then, it was outside, to one of the barns or sheds, to play the same old Cowboy and Indian games, climb trees, or sit in the tree house, watching for pirates. I would soon tire of this because I was alone, except for my dog Shep. As much as I liked Shep, hours alone with him, day after day, became boring. It just wasn't much fun. When really desperate, I would call on Arney and we would play some imaginary game. At noon, I would come in for lunch, take a short nap, then it was outside again, until Mom got home and it was time for dinner. At night, the family would sit around the radio and listen to programs like Inner Sanctum, Fibber Magee and Molly or Mr. District Attorney. Then, it was bed time. Going to sleep, I wondered what I would do the next day to make it different. On rainy days, I would either play fortress in the hay barn or stay in the house.

One day after a short rain, I was playing along the dirt-gravel road in front of the house. Lynn Lane Road, it was called. It ran north about 8 miles through farm country to Lynn Lane, a smaller community where school only went through the sixth grade. And to the south about 10 miles where miners were starting to strip-mine coal. There was seldom traffic on the narrow road so there was little danger. When a car or truck did come along, the dust plume it kicked up was enough warning to get out of the way. In a good rain, the road turned to mud and most cars would get stuck. As the rainwater flowed down the gullies on both sides of the road, I liked to catch crawdads as they came out of their holes. These were fun to play with, and occasionally, I would put one in Mary's dresser drawer. If I collected enough and saved them til the weekend, Mom would fry the tails for a Saturday breakfast. I would put them inside an old tire where they couldn't escape and feed them corn for a few days and they would make a good breakfast. Down the road about half a mile, as far as I could see, I saw another little boy playing in the road. "I wonder who that is," I said to Arney, as I headed down the road to find out.

As I got closer to the other boy, I sized him up as being about the same size and age. He was catching crawdads, too. "Whatchurname?" I asked, trying to be friendly, while at the same time trying not to appear too eager.

"Puddin' tame, puddin' tame, ask me again and I'll tell you the same," was the smart answer from the boy, who did not bother to look up from the crawdad he was examining.

"I got five marbles," I bragged, trying a different approach. "Betcha you don't have that many."

"So, what? Who cares?" came the uninterested reply.

Discouraged that the newcomer was not interested in becoming friends, I debated whether to warn him to stay out of my territory, then decided not to, and turned away to walk home. Arney and I would go play. Before I had taken half a dozen steps, the boy challenged, "Betcha I can throw a rock farther than you can." I stopped and turned around, realizing that the boy needed a friend as much as I did.

"Betcha can't" was my reply, starting the age-old ritual among small boys to determine who was best at what in order to establish a pecking order. Foot races, a jumping contest, throwing rocks at a tin can and other similar trials followed the rock-throwing competition. It is not important who won each. We finished even-steven, but that did not matter. What is important is that we were impressed enough with each other's talents, permitting formation of a friendship, one that would last through the summer. I put Arney back in my memory.

Forrest was his name. He was 6, would also start first grade in the fall, and he too had a 4-year-old sister, named Ina. He did not have any brothers. He did have a dog though, and Spot, a little smaller, got along with Shep. He and Ina had just moved into a house with their mother about a half mile south of the spot where we met - - along Lynn Lane Road, muddy in the rain, and dusty in the dry summer heat. Between our homes were just two other farm houses and the Catholic church along the mile stretch of road.

The day lasted into late afternoon, and it was soon time for dinner. Reluctantly, we split and headed in opposite directions, promising to meet the next day at my house.

Neither household had a telephone, but we managed to meet every day to play- sometimes at Forrest's, sometimes at my house, and often at the old barn halfway in between. Once in a while, we would include our sisters, especially when we were playing cavalry and needed nurses, but that was not too often. The combination of our imaginations and energies let us do a lot of things. We pooled our knowledge, and both learned. With the help of my older brother Tom, we doubled the size of the tree house and spent hours there, watching for pirates one day, and Indians the next. The hay barn on our farm would be a fort one day and a castle the next. Occasionally, our fantasies would carry us until dark and we would get home late and be in trouble, perhaps to the extent of not getting to see each other the next day.

One day, Forrest decided he wanted to ride Daisy, the Shetland pony, rumored to be more than 40 years old. I warned him that Daisy bucked, but Forrest was insistent. I held the reins while Forrest mounted bareback. Forrest took the reins and Daisy walked about 30 feet, broke into a trot, then decided she did not want a passenger. As she turned sharply and bucked, Forrest came over her head and landed in a bush. Aside from being skinned up and having a sprained wrist, Forrest was all right. That was the last time he rode Daisy.

The sprained wrist got Forrest permission to spend the night. My brother Tom was busy with something else so I got to gather eggs from the two hen houses. Forrest went with me and was impressed as I carefully gathered eggs from each of the nests. After dinner, we slept in a small tent in the back yard, listening for bears and wolves. We and the two dogs had such a good time that we decided to do it again the next week, at Forrest's house.

One time we sneaked into the milking barn late in the afternoon, with our favorite weapons, "Ys" cut from an elm tree limb with two strips of rubber, each connected on one end to a leg of the "Y", the other end to a pocket that held a green plum. - - We called them "nigger shooters," and a pocket full of green plums. I didn't know where this name came from. I had never seen a Negro, and it was not a bad word in my vocabulary. We hid behind bales of hay where we could see Bill milking one of the cows. He sat on a little "T" stool in front of the cow's rear leg, with the bucket underneath. We could hear the squirting milk hit the side of the bucket, and started shooting at him. It was like

Cowboys and Indians. He was almost finished and the bucket was almost full when a plum hit the cow in the rump. Startled, she put her hoof in the bucket, kicked it over, then kicked Bill in the leg. We would have been in big trouble if Bill had caught us, but we were faster, and his leg hurt. At the house, we got in trouble because of the loss of the milk.

I thought about sharing Arney Scroggins with Forrest, but for some reason, probably afraid that I would be teased, I didn't. So, the two never met.

One day I went to Forrest's house and he was not there. "He got bad sick during the night and I had to carry him to the hospital in Tulsa," his mother said.

"What's wrong with him?" I asked. "He was all right yesterday when we played in the tree house. Will he come home today?"

"I don't think so," his mother replied, with a worried look on her face. "He got terrible pains in his stomach last night. I took him to Johnson's down the road and we decided to carry him right to the hospital in Tulsa in their car. Doc Franklin was out of town."

Tulsa was a long way off, and there was no way I could get to the hospital to see Forrest. I missed him very much and wanted to see him badly. I went to his house each of the next three days to see if he had gotten well and come home. "No, he's not home yet. He is still very sick," she would reply. "They had to operate on him to remove his appendix."

Not knowing what that was, I had a bunch of questions which Forrest's mother answered as best as she could. "I told him you asked about him, and he smiled a little." I would wander back home aimlessly, worrying about how to fill this newly created void in my life.

On that third day, his mother said that Forrest had gotten worse. That night, Mom sat me on her lap, gave me big hug and kiss, and told me that Forrest had died. "I don't understand."

"His body was very sick. He had appendicitis and it poisoned his whole body. His spirit has left his body and gone to Heaven to live with God. He won't be sick anymore." I still didn't understand and wondered why God had taken my only friend.

"I won't have anyone to play with tomorrow," I said as the tears ran down my cheeks.

On the following day, Saturday, Mom told me to get dressed in my Sunday clothes so she could take me to see Forrest one more time. "He's back!" I thought, and the things we could do together raced through my mind.

"No," Mom replied. "You won't get to play. His spirit is gone and his body is asleep." I did not understand.

It was common during those times for viewing of the deceased to be in the home. Sort of a wake. Neither of the two funeral homes in town had viewing rooms. Mom and I walked that mile so I could see Forrest. The house was full of people dressed in black and everybody was crying. Ina looked lost and sad. Her eyes were swollen and she dabbed a tear running down her face with a hanky. At the end of the parlor was a casket resting on a stand. Spot, curled up underneath the stand, had a forlorn look on his face. Forrest looked so good lying in the casket. It was the first time I had seen him dressed up. I did not cry. I just looked at Forrest, wishing he would get up and come out and play.

Forrest was gone, and I was alone again, with no one to help chase pirates or Indians, or help defend the castle. What a short summer those 12 weeks were! But they were good ones. Now, until school started, I would have to bring Arney back into my life. The walk back home in the hot sun was miserable.

Two weeks later, Bill took me to the Morrow's Five and Dime to get my school supplies: a pencil, Big Chief tablet and a box of Crayolas. I also got a new pair of knicker pants and a shirt. I would start school in my Sunday shoes. I was ready for school. My experiences with Forrest had taught me some of the give-and-take of life which helped in making friendships. The instructions we got in the mail said I also had to get three shots from the doctor before starting school. We went to Doc Franklin's house one evening and got all three. Doc Franklin lied about those shots, saying they would not hurt. I cried all the way home.

I Went To School

I was scared on my first day of school. Mom did not take me to school, because she had to work. It probably was Tom or Bill who walked almost a mile with me, into the building, and down the hall to Miss Mary Katherine Cox's room. We lived too close to town so we couldn't ride the bus and had to walk. Spiffed up in my knickers, pullover shirt and high-top shoes, I carried a lot of stuff: my Big Chief tablet, Crayolas and pencil in a sack, and my lunch, a peanut butter and jelly sandwich and an apple wrapped in a newspaper. It was all new to me because there had been no kindergarten. Only the Baptists had kindergarten in their church, and Mom wouldn't let me go there. The summer I had just shared with Forrest prepared me for making new friends, and his sudden loss made that a necessity. I was both excited and apprehensive as it would be something new. When I walked into that room with 15 other kids, many of whom were girls, all strangers to me, I got scared. There were an equal number in the other first grade class.

Miss Cox calmed me and the others. Her stature and demeanor demanded attention. A commanding voice when she needed it, but soft. She was very soft-spoken and sugary in normal conversation, but she had a flat ruler on her desk. She made me sit on the front row. I wondered if she saw me as a problem child. I did not think I was, but learned to be at times. My formal education, which would last the next 16 years, had begun. Dad had told me to behave myself, and that if I ever got a whippin' at school, I would get another when I got home. That thought stayed with me through high school.

About 20 of the kids who walked through the doors into those two first-grade classes for the first time that day composed 40 percent of my graduating class 12 years later. There were Jean, Mayze, Bill, John Dale and others. So it was not only a beginning in formal education, it was also the beginning of establishing friendships and acquaintances that lasted years, many of which still exist today.

Miss Cox was pretty and a nice lady, and was extremely good at handling any fears we had. The ruler on her desk would also strike fear in the heart occasionally.

I noticed girls for the first time. The only ones I really knew up to that time were my sister and Forrest's sister Ina. I think I noticed girls because they didn't play ball with us boys at recess. There was Gwilda Davis, who became my favorite. She was a rather plump little girl with long, golden brown hair worn in Shirley Temple curls. She was the daughter of the junior high school principal. Gwilda liked me. Mayze Walker was a freckle-faced "tomboy" who could keep up with any of the boys. John Dale McCuistion looked to be the biggest boy in the class. I would have to make friends with him. Bobby Smith might be a nice friend.

About halfway through learning the ABC's, I got sick and spent some time in the hospital--had my tonsils removed. That seems to have been a cure for a lot of ails--"Well, he's got a cold. Let's remove his tonsils. And while we're at it, we'll remove his adenoids." Doc Franklin would say. Sooner or later, everybody had their tonsils removed. Now, it's rarely done, but when done, it is routine--in and out of the hospital, oftentimes in the same day.

Then, it was different. When you went in the hospital, you could figure on at least a week. It didn't seem to make any difference how minor the problem. Then, there was a recovery period. My case of tonsils was even more complex. I came out of the hospital (from Tulsa--we didn't have one in Broken Arrow), and the first or second night at home, I started hemorrhaging in my sleep. I don't remember the events of that night--it's a hazy nightmare. I don't know who woke me up, but it was probably Tom, sleeping next to me. I don't know who took me to the doctor, or how we got there as there was no car. I do remember blood all over the pillow and sheet. Ole Doc Franklin may have even made a house call. If I hadn't gotten to a doctor, I would probably have either choked or bled to death. I almost did the latter anyway.

I still remember--and that's the nightmare of it--Doc Franklin poking those swabs down my throat to stop the bleeding. It hurts today to think of it. The doctor in Tulsa who did the operation--I can't remember his name now --was a very nice man, Mom thought he was a butcher for letting me bleed like that.

I missed most of a month of school, and after that, it was good to be back and see Gwilda and Miss Cox. I was kind of a national hero coming back, almost like returning from the dead. Everybody was glad to see me--glad to know I was among the living--and healthy. I remember getting two special hugs that made the whole thing worthwhile. Miss Cox gave me a big one, and right behind her was Gwilda. She even added a kiss on the cheek. I was teased a lot by the boys, but I know they were just envious.

Miss Cox and Gwilda, my tonsils, and the fact that I passed first grade are still in my memory. I was really proud of passing the first grade. Miss Cox moved after that year, and Gwilda moved about three years later.

The War

We were almost halfway through the second grade when the Japanese bombed Pearl Harbor, Army, Navy and Air Corps installations in Hawaii, a territory of the United States. It was the beginning of World War II. I was 7 and halfway through the second grade. For the next five years, I watched the war progress through the eyes of a young boy. I had a picture of General Douglas Macarthur on my wall. He was my favorite war hero, but I always thought how strange that someone would name a boy "General." "Remember Pearl Harbor" was our slogan throughout the war. In the living room, there were pictures of Mike and Bill in uniform, Jack Scissons in his Royal Canadian Air Force uniform, and cousins Don Eustice, a Navy ensign, and Hank and Pat Southwood, both in the Army.

In 1943 and 1944, I saw brothers Mike and Bill go off to the war, and we proudly displayed the 2-star flag in our window. These flags, with the blue star on a white background, were abundant around town. The star indicated a resident of the home was in the military service. We prayed daily that we would never have to replace those blue stars with gold ones, indicating the person had died while in service.

Mike sent me a white sailor hat that I could wear in his honor. It was way too big for me but I wore it everywhere. About every two weeks. Mom would throw it in the laundry, depriving me of it for a day or two. As soon as it was dry - - sometimes still a little damp, it was back on my head.

It was a time of intense patriotism. Our freedom was threatened and we all had to do our part. "Lucky Strike Green Has Gone to War," we

"Buttoned our Lip to Save a Ship," Uncle Sam pointed that finger at us in posters everywhere, asking us to do our part; and it was "V-dot-dot-dot-dash," V for victory. Nylons disappeared, and cigarettes, gasoline and tires, as well as many other things, were rationed on a coupon basis. Mom went to work in the Douglas bomber plant. She paid for her bus transportation to work with a portion of our gas coupons. The rest were used for farm equipment. Since she didn't smoke, she traded our cigarette coupons for other things.

Birthday and Christmas presents became government savings stamps in different denominations to support the war effort. One Christmas, one of my favorite gifts was a dime bank from my Aunt Rose. It would hold 50 dimes. I would fill it, then trade dimes for savings stamps. How excited and proud we were to paste them into a book not unlike a Green Stamp book. Then, when full, we would turn it in at the Post Office in exchange for an $18.75 war bond. In seven years, the bond was redeemable for $25. There was a school-sponsored program where we could take a dime or quarter in weekly, and place it in a slot of a cardboard jacket. When it was full, we would exchange it for savings stamps. The school provided certificates of recognition. Years later, those war bonds, tucked away in Mom's secret file, helped pay for my college education.

We did our part in other ways. A continuous scrap metal drive existed throughout the war. All this scrap metal would be turned into guns, bullets, tanks and ships. The school, scout troops, churches, civic clubs and other groups picked up this drive. We picked metal up wherever we could find it and turned it in. There was always a place to take it. If it wasn't tied down, we would take it. If we couldn't move it, we would get help. We would get credit for it by the pound, and when we got so many pounds, we would get a certificate. We would save tin foil from cigarette packs and gum wrappers and roll it into a ball. We would peel if off the paper, and apply it to the ball. When it got big enough, we would turn it in at school.

Savings bond drives came to town, bringing soldiers and sailors who had been "there" and were returning--some wounded--to ask us to keep up the good work and do our part. In 1944, after being awarded the Medal of Honor for service with the 45th Infantry Division in Italy, Lt. Ernest Childers, a Broken Arrow Creek Indian, came home for a celebration in his honor. For various amounts of savings stamps or bonds purchased, or scrap collected, one would get a ride in a real army jeep with Lt. Childers. I wore my "too big" sailor hat all the time.

At Saturday afternoon movies, we'd watch the latest edition of "Movietone News," which told us how the war was going. I remember shopping with Mom, and the first question always asked when she saw a friend went something like, "How do you think the war is going?" And each would relate their concerns about the latest news, or what the last letter from the boy at the front said. Correspondence from service men was slow. To receive a letter written a month ago, then censored, was common. "A month ago, Mike was at sea, in the Pacific, someplace," was a common response.

Our childhood games turned, for the most part, into "war games." With homemade guns of scrap wood, we were always landing on some beach head, or climbing into the imaginary cockpit of a P-40 or P-51 fighter to shoot down the dirty Japs and Germans. Cowboys and Indians were set aside for the "duration." The sacrifices everybody had to make would be for the "duration of the war." That was soon shortened to the "duration," which would come to mean six months after the war ended.

There was a brand of cigarette named Wings. Each pack had a picture of the latest U.S. fighter or bomber. The only one I knew who smoked Wings was our school crossing guard at the corner of Main and College, where the elementary school was. We kids would catch him every morning, taking turns to get the picture he had saved for us. A Wings card collection was more important than baseball cards. Lucky Strike cigarettes came in a green pack. About 1942-43, the pack was changed to white and the promotion was "Lucky Strike Green has gone to war," to be used in camouflage uniforms.

Not long after the war began, we began to see the Hollywood version at the NuShow. "Colin Kelly," one of our first heroes, had crashed his plane into a Japanese battleship, and we saw it on the screen. We saw the death march at Bataan, Corregidor, and Wake Island, etc. John Wayne was really good. He was a foot soldier, a Marine pilot, and a Navy ship captain. How versatile he was. *Thirty Seconds over Tokyo* told of our first heroic bombing raid over Tokyo. These all had a big part in our lives. Morale in the country was at a low ebb because of Pearl Harbor and the Japanese sweep across the Pacific, as well as what was going on in Europe. *Remember Pearl Harbor* was a slogan used throughout the war. These movies fanned the flames of patriotism, and kept the war effort at the forefront of our thinking. It made all those sacrifices easier.

On occasion, hundreds and hundreds of planes, it seemed like, flying in formation, would dot the sky overhead at one time, being ferried to some debarkation air base for service in the war. I would lie on the ground, watching them, and fantasize being the pilot of one of them. Then, it was always back to the barn "airplane" to help them.

During the last year of the war, and for a couple of years after, Dad worked as a volunteer counselor for the VFW helping returning veterans in the readjustment process: things like getting their benefits arranged, finding a place to live, getting back in school, and getting any required medical treatment. When one of them would come to the house, I would sit in awe, looking at this hero and listening to war stories.

In the march across Germany, my cousin, Pat Southwood, was killed in action. He was awarded the Silver Star, and was buried in Germany, then his body was returned home after the war. I got to be an altar boy at his funeral mass.

Then, one day, May 7, 1945, Germany surrendered the war was over in Europe. We called it VE Day, A neighbor was to take Mary and I to a movie that night but the theater was closed in celebration. It seemed that everybody was in town celebrating. Car and air horns honked continually through the night. Then, we dropped the big bombs on Hiroshima and Nagasaki and Japan surrendered on August 14, and we celebrated VJ Day. The war was over. President Roosevelt didn't get to see this. He had died a few months earlier, and was succeeded by Harry Truman, who had to make that decision about the atomic bomb. The boys began coming home--at least most of them. There were celebrations and parades for a long time. Many didn't come home.

Getting out of the service to come home as a civilian was determined by a point system. Not everyone could come home at once. Points were awarded for time in service, rank, campaigns fought, decorations, wounds, etc. When one accumulated the required number of points, he was discharged. We tried to keep track of Mike's and Bill's points on a daily basis. They finally had enough and came home. We went to the train station in Broken Arrow to meet Mike and proudly escorted him home. The war was over for us.

Many of the returning boys, although not Mike or Bill, had quit high school to go serve their country. Getting back in school was difficult for both them and the school population. But it was awfully nice to have a couple of war-hardened veterans on the high school football team.

Dad, holding me, with Mike,
Tom and Bill, circa 1935

Mom, with Mary and me
Circa 1938

Grandmother Eustice with us
Circa 1937

Mary and I on Daisy
Circa 1940

St. Anne's Catholic Church

Collecting Scrap Metal
for the War Circa 1943

A Gift For Suzanne

In my early years in school, it was always a custom to draw names at Christmas time for exchange of gifts at a classroom party held the last school day before the holidays. Each room had its own tree with all the presents under it, and there were always decorated Christmas cookies, fruit cake and punch, brought by homeroom mothers, so it was a festive occasion.

It must have been the second or third grade when I had a crush appropriate to that age for one of the prettiest girls in the class. Suzanne was part Creek Indian and had the traditional Indian features--dark complexion, dark flashing eyes, and long, jet black hair. She had a pretty smile.

I don't think Suzanne knew I existed. That didn't make any difference. When it came to name drawing, I wanted her name. When we drew for names, I didn't get it. First, I had to find out who had it, then arrange a swap. We weren't supposed to tell whose name we got, but there were ways of finding out. I finally located the boy who had Suzanne's name, but he wasn't interested in the name I had drawn so it ended up in a four-way swap. I traded to someone else, then traded that name for one acceptable to the boy who had Suzanne's. It was a masterpiece of horsetrading, but I got her name, and it was worth it.

Now, I had to find a gift that would really impress her. I think there was a 50-cent limit. I looked and looked, and looked. I couldn't find anything for her that seemed appropriate. I had looked through all the aisles at Morrow's 5 and Dime store. I just wasn't a good shopper. I often wished I hadn't gone to the trouble to get her name. I didn't know what I was going to do. I had no help. Tom was four years older and had bigger problems to worry about. Mary was two years younger--too young to know anything. Because of work, Mom was not available, and I couldn't ask Dad. At the last moment, when the pressures and frustrations were really bearing down, I, out of desperation, bought her a big red rubber ball.

Mom helped me to wrap it, and tie a ribbon around it. It looked pretty, but I learned that there is just not much room for imagination in wrapping a rubber ball. I took it to school and put it under the tree. I was proud, but I had some reservations. Was it the right present for her? I was also excited, probably more so because it was over and the pressure was off.

Finally, the last school day before the holidays arrived, and we fidgeted all day long waiting for the last hour--the time of the party. Everybody was dressed to the best, which added to the holiday atmosphere. A teacher from another class dressed as Santa, and a couple of students were picked to be his helpers.

I watched Suzanne get her gift, and start to open it. I was so excited. Off came the paper and there was the red rubber ball. She looked across at me as I watched her--there was no pretty smile. It was really a good thing the Indian Wars were long past. Suzanne did not speak to me for at least two years. We became friends again during our later school years, but the crush had been destroyed.

If I would have gotten her a set of jacks to go with the ball, or perhaps a bottle of perfume, things may have been different.

OurReligion

As I said earlier, we were all raised in the Catholic faith. Mom and Dad were devout. The Connery family in the late 30s had donated two acres of road frontage to the south of our house to build a church. A little stone church was torn down in Jenks, about 10 miles away, and rebuilt on that property. St. Anne's Parish was dedicated in 1937 and Father Joseph Griffin came to be our priest. When World War II started in 1941, Father Griffin joined the Army Chaplain Corps, and went off to war.

The following is not intended to be a condemnation of the Catholic Church. Neither is it intended to throw stones at the non-Catholic population of Broken Arrow. Although the church provided for all of our spiritual needs, it was tough growing up Catholic. When this would come up, we were always reminded of the early Christian martyrs, and that we should "carry the cross" as they did.

At that time, the Catholic population in Oklahoma was less than 3 percent. In Broken Arrow, it was less than that. We were defined as being in mission territory. The majority of people in Broken Arrow worshipped at the Assembly of God, First Baptist, or Methodist Church. There were about 15 other protestant churches to accommodate 3,000 people. Social groupings centered primarily around the church. There were social groupings in the school system, i.e. band, football, FFA, home ec, etc. For youth however, primary groupings evolved from the church. Baptists socialized with Baptists, Presbyterians with Presbyterians. Adjacent to the church were Christian organizations. There was Demolay, a Christian organization for young men. A strong chapter existed in Broken Arrow. For the girls, there was Rainbow Girls, a Masonic organization for young women. These groups were strong and well attended in town. However, young Catholic men and women could not belong to these groups. I always thought that we were excluded by the organizations, but it may have been that the Catholic church said "No" to them. In either case, we were outsiders. There were only John Rodgers, a classmate of mine who lived on a bigger farm, farther out in the country, and my sister Mary. Growing up, we had little social life, except with those groups formed in school.

We learned our religion well in catechism classes on Saturday. There was a period of time when a nun or two would come from a convent in Tulsa to teach us. I never could understand why we didn't have Sunday school like my friends had. In time, we went to our first confession and communion, and received the sacraments of Penance and Holy Communion. In junior high, when we got a priest after the war, I learned the Latin prayers, learned what they meant, became an altar boy and served Mass on Sunday. John Rodgers and I took turns. As a teenager, I also ushered and took up the offering. I remember my Aunt Bebe, one of Dad's spinster sisters who lived in the barn apartment, accused me of rattling the coins in the collection basket as I passed it.

The Catholic Church was very conservative. We were taught that we had the inside track to Heaven, and that we should always pray for the conversion of all non-Catholics. At the end of the Mass, we said prayers for the conversion of Russia. Whether religious or not, they were all but doomed. The Baptists and all the others resented us for that. "Who were we to be 'holier than thou?'" They brought their lack of understanding to bear. We were reminded often that our priests were alcoholic, and that they slept with nuns. That was for starters. We were about one step ahead of the Negroes in social structure, who had to be out of town by sundown.

About the age of 12, I knew a girl, about 8, who lived with her single mother along my paper route. Her mother had a live-in boyfriend. I made the statement to a friend one day that they were going to Hell. It was dogmatic, judgmental, and there was no place for argument.

My religion taught me that. I have always remembered making that statement and have regretted it.

Once in elementary school, I was selected to be a shepherd in the school Christmas play. My parents wouldn't let me be in it because it was to be held in the First Baptist Church. In the summer of 1944, between the fourth and fifth grade, the school auditorium burned, taking with it a few classrooms. When school started that fall, we went to school in the basement of the Methodist Church, which was across the street. Mother really had problems with that.

When Father Griffin left for the army, we did not get a replacement priest. We went through the four years of war without one. Occasionally, a visiting priest would come through. Anyone interested could gather on Sunday evening to say the Rosary. Once in a great while, we got to go to Tulsa to Mass. This was really a treat because we didn't have a car, and there were too many of us to go together with someone else. Many of the parishioners seemed to disappear. Some moved--others fell away from the church. We became a pretty small group. We never filled the church on Sunday. It was always filled at Midnight Mass on Christmas Eve because many of the townspeople, curiosity seekers, would come out to see what was going on. The Ritchie girl from Jenks, where we always bought our Christmas and Thanksgiving turkeys, would come over for Midnight Mass and sing, *O Holy Night* or *Ave Maria*.

Pat Moore and his parents joined us and lived west of town in my junior year, but Pat, a grade behind me, continued in a Catholic school in Tulsa. That same year, Joan Monroe, who was Mary's age, moved to town. (She later became Mary's sister-in-law.) Now, there were five of us. We still did not have much social life because we lived so far apart, but we always got together after Mass on Sunday. We were always subject to cajoling, teasing, and name calling by many of those we considered to be friends. I remember a group of guys giving me a bad time one time, and one of them said, "Not only is he Catholic, but he's adopted too." That caused me concern for awhile.

One time I invited a new friend to come home with me after school and play. Wayne Peters was his name. We played the afternoon in the barn and had a good time. He told me he was Lutheran. I knew where the Lutheran church was because I passed it on my morning paper route. I told Mom about him that night, and she asked me not to see him again.

"Why?" I asked.

"He's Lutheran," she replied. "That means he's German. We are at war with Germany," she continued. "They are our enemy." That was that. Wayne continued to be a distant closet friend, but we never went to each other's house again.

After the end of WWII, we thought Father Griffin would return, but he was assigned elsewhere. In about 1947, we received Father Wenceslas, a priest from Poland, who had been in a German concentration camp during the war. Then another came, and another. The church began to grow, aided by movement of the American Airlines maintenance facility from New York to Tulsa, and by 1952, ground had been broken for an elementary school. St. Anne's (the old rock church has been replaced by a more-modern church) became the headquarters for their order, and they have a monastery there along with a school. Stories about living with, interacting with, and worshiping with these Polish priests would fill a book in and of itself.

One time, Father Wenceslas came to the house extremely excited. "We're getting a organ," he said in his broken English. "New York is sending an organ to us." His order had procured an organ for us from a church in New York that was being torn down. The parish was so excited and awaited anxiously for this event. Finally, it arrived - - a pipe organ so large that it took a flatbed trailer and semi-truck to haul the pipes. There were so many pipes and they were so long that they would not stand in our little church. The organ ended up in our hay barn and remained there for several years. We kidded Father Wenceslas about setting it up in our front yard.

Time finally caught up with us and Mary and I needed to go through confirmation. Mary and I were already two or three years older that the average confirmand. Only the Bishop (of both Oklahoma City and Tulsa) could confirm, and it was decided that we would be confirmed at Christ the King Church in Tulsa, parish church of Aunt Rose (Dad's sister), who lived two blocks from the church. We would base out of her home, get our final instructions and go through confirmation with the class at Marquette, the parish school. To this day I remember sitting with that class at confirmation, at least a head taller than anyone else and a couple of years older, hunkering down in our pew, fearful the Bishop was going to ask one of us a question.

About twice a year, the church would have a rummage sale. I don't think anybody had garage sales in those days. Other variations such as boot sales and yard sales were not common either. Maybe people just didn't want the public to see the old clothes or junk they had to sell. Rummage sales were collections of goods brought by congregation members to sell to the public, with profits going to a building fund, altar guild or perhaps to buy new hymnals. In advance of these sales, Mom would instruct us boys to gather the things we couldn't (wouldn't) wear any more. There was never much in our home because when one boy couldn't wear something, it went down a notch to the next, finally ending up with me, if it lasted that long. By the time I finished with it, the rag-bag was the next destination. It was different with Mary. Although she inherited occasional items from cousins in Tulsa, they were usually good enough for one more wear after she was through. On Saturday, the stuff would be spread across the church yard with price labels attached: a nickel for this, twenty five cents for that. The economy of the times kept many folks out of the new item stores and brought them to rummage sales. At the end of the day, the money would be counted and the remaining stuff stored in a room of Father's house, next to the church.

One day, Mom came home quite proud of herself. "John, I bought you a new shirt and pair of pants. They go well together. You'll be able to wear them to school. Come try them on," she said. "I got them both for fifty cents." Carefully, I looked at the shirt and pants on a hanger.

"Mom, these are the same pants and shirt I gave you yesterday to take to the sale."

"At least, we know they came from a good family," she replied, as she went into hysterical laughter, laughing at herself.

Mom had always hoped the church would grow, a school be established, and that it would be constructed on what was our property.

All farming had ceased and Mary's horse, Pete, and Rudy, the dog, were the only animals occupying the property. In 1955, when the property got too big for her (there were just Mom and Mary at home), she sold the property to the church at an excellent price, with that expectation. Within a year or two, the church sold the property, doubling their money, and bought property to the south of the church. That caused Mom--and all of us--a lot of heartache, but her faith never wavered. Years later, the church bought back the lower half of the property and built a large gym.

When I went to college, the University of Oklahoma, I felt strong in my faith. I joined Theta Kappa Phi, Catholic men's fraternity, and was active in the Newman Club, a social club for Catholic students. Catholic numbers were few on that campus of 18,000 students, six times larger than my hometown population. It just didn't make sense to me that all of these students, most of them good people, were going to Hell. However, I continued to pray for them every Sunday.

Tastes Great? Less Filling?

A beer company did an advertising commercial once where it had two sides of its followers arguing with each other. One shouted "Tastes Great," while the other countered with "Less Filling." They may both have been right.

In the 1930s, things were much simpler. Dad liked a good beer, but he always brewed his own. During the war years, he traded ration stamps to get all the ingredients necessary to make a batch. I'm told that his beer always tasted great and was in demand by neighbors. He would brew it and let it age in the hay barn. Once in a great while, he would cap a batch too soon and the bottles would blow, leaving the barn smelling like a beer hall. Mom would occasionally drink a beer. Her favorite alcoholic drink was Mogen David wine. I don't remember them ever drinking stronger alcoholic drinks. In the evenings of those hot summer days, Dad liked to relax in the glider in the back yard and drink one of his beers.

Dad always told my older brothers, as they got to the right age, that if and when they wanted to start drinking, to start at home. He realized they would grow up, and would try it sooner or later, with or without his blessing. With the war on, and knowing they would enlist in the service after high school graduation he knew that they would be soon out of his influence and subject to many outside influences, such as drinking and smoking. With this and other teaching, he would prepare them for the world they would face. He was never able to do that for me, because when I got to that age, he had died.

When they started drinking beer, the only thing I knew about it was that it must be good, for they would forsake lemonade, ice tea and other cold drinks for a beer. Beer came in brown bottles so it was easily identifiable.

One Saturday, I was helping Mom do the laundry. Monday was the traditional wash day, but since Mom worked outside the home, it had to be done on weekends. More than likely, I was just in the way. The washing machine, an old wringer type, was in the basement, and she hung the clothes out on a line in the back yard to dry. Everything, after coming out of the washer, went through two rinse tubs, was run through the hand operated wringer, then hung out. So, there were some things this little boy could do, even though it may be only moving clothes about. I wasn't allowed to run the wringer.

The basement served other functions as well. There were shelves on one wall which always seemed full of homemade canned goods: canned pork, beef, green beans, peas, corn and tomatoes. All were canned in the summer and would get us through the winter. At the other end was a jerry-rigged butter churn, operated by an electric motor. The canister held about three gallons of cream, and when we had enough to fill it, we made butter. At the opposite end was a sump pump in the floor to handle water in case of flooding. The basement was also our "fraidy hole," shelter from the dreaded tornado. I remember using it only once for that purpose.

Mom had gone out to hang out a load of clothes, while I sat on the floor, sorting a pile of dirty clothes. I saw this brown bottle on the shelf, and quickly decided this was my chance to find out what beer was all about. I would be able to hear her coming down the stairs, and would have time to get it back without her knowing.

I took a big swallow, and boy, did it taste bad. I must have choked, coughed and sputtered for two or three minutes. There is no way I could understand why anyone would drink that stuff. There had to be some saving grace about it, because Mike and Bill seemed to like it. "Don't give up too soon," I thought to myself," and took another big swallow. It tasted worse than the first, although it went down a little easier.

I thought I would give it one more try. As I started to tip the bottle up, Mom came down the stairs. I didn't hear her coming. It's a good thing she caught me.

She screamed, grabbed the bottle from my hand, picked me up by the shirt and pulled me up the stairs, through the back porch and into the kitchen. I knew I was going to get a good whippin'. I didn't. She saw the problem right away. I had been drinking Clorox. Things got a little tense for a few moments. I don't know what Doc Franklin told her on the phone, but the next thing I knew, she was pouring something warm--I don't know what--down my throat. I soon threw up; then she did it again, and again, and again.

I suppose if she hadn't reacted as soon as she did, the insides of my stomach would have eaten through. My stomach and throat burned for days. I've always thought that because of that, I have a cast iron stomach, and can handle anything.

For a long time, I thought it was because of me that they started putting clorox in white bottles. And it's only in the hottest of weather that I drink a beer.

My Relationship With Dad

In later years, my brother Mike and I discussed parts of this book, and the subject turned to Dad. Mike commented that life must have been pretty tough for Mary and me during Dad's last years. "In fact," Mike asked, "Couldn't Dad be arrested today for child abuse?" I would not answer that question.

1936 was his last year of good health, and perhaps one of the better years of his life. After Dad fathered four boys, Mary Margaret was born on August 1. He was extremely proud and delighted to have a girl in the family. That was the year he received the WWI Veterans bonus and he bought a new Ford Model T farm truck, the only vehicle owned by the Connerys.

He had "Arrow Farms" painted on the doors of his new Model T. During the early morning, he would deliver vegetables, eggs and, occasionally, a quart of milk to his customers around town. Later that year, when his health began to fail, he decided he needed to teach Mom to drive. She had never been behind the wheel. He thought that our driveway, which came in from Lynn Lane Road along the north property boundary, curved to the right along the side of the house, around the hay barn and back out to Lynn Lane, would be a good place to learn. The 300-foot gravel stretch that came in from the road was bounded on the north by a barbed wire fence, and on the south by a row of five or six large elm trees. Mom did fine in her early lessons, including driving in a circle around the barn, but the last time, on the straight stretch, she lost control of the truck, skidded off the drive and hit three of the elm trees before she could stop. Fortunately, her physical injuries were minor, but she was extremely frightened to the point that she never got behind the wheel again. The trees survived but the truck was totaled.

Dad's health continued to decline. During the next four years, he was in one of three VA hospitals more than at home. He was diagnosed with TB, attributed to weakened lungs from being gassed in WWI. He went through major surgery at Hines VA hospital in Chicago, where one lung and part of the other were removed along with several ribs to arrest the disease. He spent rehabilitation years in VA hospitals in Muskogee and Sulphur, OK.

During this rehabilitation, he had to take up a hobby, doing something with his hands. He selected leather crafting. Using the finest leather available, he learned to make wallets and purses, creating an artistic design on each. One Christmas, we boys received hand-tooled wallets, each with our initials. Mom and Mary received purses. Each of us used them for several years. Some of these items are still around, relics of his work in the 1930s.

Dad lived the rest of his life almost as an invalid. He coughed continually, often spitting up much phlegm to clear his remaining lung. He was often sick, often in pain, had very little patience, and wasn't tolerant at all. He moved to the back bedroom, where his coughing would not disturb Mom. Dad was quick to punish, and he punished hard, usually with the strap he used to sharpen his straight razor. I remember, he would say, "I'm gonna slap you up to a peak, then slap the peak off." This became a way of life.

At times, when he thought one of us was deserving of a whippin', he would say, "I don't have time right now. Remind me tonight and I'll spank you." That made for a really hard day, and it would take him forever to drag that reminder out of me, but he always did. "Weren't you supposed to remind me of something tonight?" he would ask.

When I was small, 2 perhaps 3, I had long blondish red hair which was filled with curls. I was Daddy's little curly top. I was closer to him then than I ever was again. That was before he got sick.

Mary and I were afraid of him. When we wanted to go someplace, or do something together, we would argue for what seemed like hours as to who would have to ask Dad. We were always afraid of his reaction, and the possible "No" we would get.

One day--I guess I was about 11--Mom, Dad and I were in the kitchen. Dad was cooking hamburgers in a skillet. I don't remember what we were talking about, but I made some smart aleck remark to Mom. In a flash, he raised the spatula out of the skillet and slapped me across the face with it, greasy and hot. Not a word was said. This left burn marks across my face for a week. He got my attention. He demanded the utmost respect for Mom.

When I was about 13, and getting ready for a week at scout camp, we found that there weren't enough counselors, and the trip might be canceled. Dad volunteered. Dad went, and had a good time. He did much of the cooking, and enjoyed that, but it was a tiring experience for him. That's one of the few times I can remember Dad doing things that boys liked to do, at least with me. I was really proud that he went, and I thoroughly enjoyed the experience, even though it cramped my style a bit. That was the summer before he died. When he was physically able, he liked to hunt, especially quail. He and Tom would go frequently during the season. He did take me rabbit hunting one winter day. What I remember about that day was his teaching me to unload the shotgun before going over a barbed wire fence.

Tom, four years older, was always much closer to Dad than I was--at least it seemed that way. I guess it should have been that way as Tom worked harder and was more responsible. Tom grew up calling Dad "Pop." I always wanted to be that familiar with him, and I envied Tom, but I never felt like I was good enough.

Dad came to my defense one time when I was about 10. I was riding my bike into an intersection, making a right turn, when I got hit by a pickup driving on the wrong side of the street. I had eased around the stop sign right into his path. Dad got angry at the other driver, and it was that anger that got me a rebuilt bike. His support meant a lot to me. I guess you could say that when the chips were down, he got in your corner.

As you'll see later, Tom could--and would--get me in trouble with Dad. Granted, a lot of it I did all by myself--Tom just blew the whistle--but I don't think Tom ever covered for me unless it involved us both. Dad always seemed to take Tom's word at face value, and what I said didn't matter. He was quick to punish but very poor at counseling.

Dad rolled his own cigarettes. He smoked Prince Albert, and always had the red can in his pocket along with an orange package of cigarette papers. He could roll them about as good as the next guy, but they never looked anything like what came out of a pack. They would flake and come apart as he smoked, like embers from a fire, and I don't think he had a shirt or pair of trousers that didn't have burn holes in it. His favorite chair, a red upholstered pedestal rocker, was covered with burn spots. I remember one Christmas, or perhaps a birthday, when I bought him a cigarette roller. I thought surely he would use it as it did a much better job, but I don't think he ever did. Later, Tom and I would use it when we would occasionally sneak a smoke.

Because Dad always had much pain in his back where the ribs had been removed, one of us gave him an alcohol rubdown at night. I enjoyed doing that, because it made me feel closer to him, and I could bring him some relief. He had to work hard to keep his one lung cleared of phlegm. If he could keep it clear, he could breathe. So, he carried a sputum cup to use when needed, and that was often. He would order these by the gross, and always had a spare close at hand. Dad's pockets were always full. Between his Prince Albert, rolling papers, cup, wallet and handkerchief and a handful of stick matches, he couldn't carry anything else.

As much as possible, Dad was active in the Lions Club. He took me and a friend of mine as guests to one of the meetings. It may have been a Father-Son luncheon--I don't recall, but I was proud to be there with him.

Dad could fix about anything--or make anything--when there was not a lot of physical labor involved. He was so bony though, and his veins were so close to the surface, that he couldn't do anything without bleeding.

Not long before Christmas, 1949, Dad got sick again and returned to the hospital in Muskogee, about 50 miles away. He had heart problems, and had trouble breathing. He always seemed congested, a fallout from the tuberculosis, and having only 1/4ᵗʰ of normal lung capacity. He was 56 years old. He would hallucinate and was not always conscious of what was going on around him. He accused Mom of stealing his money, which broke her heart, even though she understood his condition. I didn't understand his condition, and because of that, I became angry with him. Although he never knew it, that anger was with me a long time.

Mom became special to me. All of my friends had moms who were in the home. Whenever I went to one of the homes, their Mom was there. My mom never was. She was still at work, 20 miles away in Tulsa, and didn't get home until about 6. Like my friends, I wanted mom to be home when I got there, so, I would delay coming home. I'd find some place, usually Jack Hudson's, to stop and play ball during my paper route. Then I would finish delivering the rest of my papers then go home, arriving after Mom was home. I did not realize I could have made life much easier on her if I had delivered my papers and gone right home. I could have had all my chores done by the time she got home. But, I didn't. I just did not realize.

The Front Yard

We always had a large front yard, rimmed with large elm and maple trees, and in the spring, it was beautiful. It was 80 yards deep from Lynn Lane Road (I remember because at one time, I laid out an 80 yard football field with yard markers and no end zone) and about 40 yards wide. Sections of pasture were on either side, a barbed wire fence on one side and an electric fence on the north pasture section. North of that was a long driveway, which came in from Lynn Lane, looped around between the hay barn and house, around the back side of the barn and back to the road.

The back yard was perhaps one-fourth as big when one considered all the close trim work required. This became a real challenge to mow in summer--and it was mowed once a week. Dad insisted. To let it go much longer than that would make it difficult to mow with what we had. A good part of the front, at least the pasture sections, was dotted with elm and maple trees. We always whitewashed them in the summer, so the yard was pretty. Dad insisted it be kept that way.

There was no such thing as a power mower in my early years. Even if there were, you couldn't get gasoline during the war. We had a reel push mower. There was no way the yard could be kept up with just that.

We also had a Shetland pony, named Daisy. She had been given to us when Mike and Bill were little boys. When I was a young teenager, this pony was over 40 years old, so we were told. We rode the pony as kids--Mary did much more so than I. Daisy had a mind of her own, and after she threw me a couple of times, I lost complete interest.

Dad thought Daisy could help mow the yard. He fashioned a

harness for her that had a swivel connection which hooked to the push mower. It worked. Mary and I became the chief lawn mower operators--one to ride Daisy, the other to walk behind and guide the lawnmower. We would switch off frequently, and surprisingly enough, the whole yard could be mowed in a day. We would argue occasionally about who had to do what. Although I didn't care that much about riding Daisy, it was better than walking behind the mower.

In my younger school years, after I was in school and began to develop friends, the yard became a tremendous play yard. On summer days, kids would gather after dinner as it cooled off. We were isolated, but kids came from everywhere, it seemed. We even designated a place to park bikes. We had two to three hours before dark to play. Blind Man's Bluff, Kick the Can, Hide and Seek, and Red Rover were popular games. Where teams were involved, we would pick "captains" and choose up sides. We would use a baseball bat to determine who would choose first.

If a game involved hiding places, there were plenty around the barns and behind shrubs. It was always difficult to quit as it got dark. But there was always tomorrow. As we got older, the yard was set up for football games on Saturday or Sunday afternoon. Since there was no Pop Warner football in Broken Arrow, a game usually started by choosing up sides. Gene Karnes formed a team on the west side of town and they would come play a team we formed. In the fall, we would imitate on Saturday what we saw the Broken Arrow Tigers do Friday night. We would get Tom to bring his classmates, who played high school football to help coach our sandlot teams. Most of the time, we would play touch, but occasionally, we'd go all out and play tackle.

Football was a big sport in Broken Arrow. The town would close down on Friday night to come see the Tigers play, whether they were at home, or at Claremore, Skiatook, Pawhuska or elsewhere. It always seemed to me that Friday night at 9 o'clock would be the best time to rob the First National or Arkansas River bank, because there was no one in town, even Gene Flowers, the policeman. They all were at the football game.

Jack Hudson, a year behind me, also had a big yard. He lived on

College Street, about halfway between the high school and downtown. Boys would gather there after school for football or baseball. There were many times, I would get wooed onto his yard for a little football when my paper route took me down College Street. Sometimes, that would get me into trouble because customers would complain about late delivery. Jack grew up to be the high school quarterback his junior and senior year, then went on to play at Vanderbilt.

Mary and I were doing so well with the yard, and when we began to raise fewer and fewer cattle as Mike, Bill, and Tom left home, we decided to turn the section of pasture bordering the driveway into yard. That doubled the size of the front, and that gave us room to play baseball. I was never a serious baseball player, or basketball player for that matter. These were both popular sports in Broken Arrow, but not like football. There would always be American Legion baseball and the town would have a team. I tried out for shortstop, and one day a hot grounder took a bad hop and hit me in the nose, ending my baseball career.

After the war, we went "uptown" and, for awhile, had a power reel mower, with a Briggs and Stratton motor. Although it was good, it took almost as much time as Daisy, but at least one person could operate it. Then we got a Yazoo rotary power mower. It had to be pushed, and it didn't cut the grass as well, but it was faster.

The yard, and its appearance, was always important to us. It was beautiful through my childhood. It was usable also. The large amount of room made for some interesting games. The back yard was nice also. We had a rope swing on a cross bar between two posts, a lawn glider and a large number of shade trees. It offered many hiding places for use when we played those games. We spent many evenings in the summer and fall enjoying the yard. And it was also a workplace. I remember the many hours during the summer when Mom, Mary and I, and sometimes Tom, would sit in that glider snapping beans, shelling peas or husking corn from the garden, all to be canned for the winter.

It was discouraging to go back in later years, find the house torn down and a 12-14 unit apartment house standing in our front yard. What's the old saying, "You can never go home again?"

Delivering Papers

Delivering newspapers was a way of life around the Connery household. Three older brothers delivered the Tulsa World or Tribune ahead of me. By the time it got to me, we had the whole town. There were about three routes for the Tulsa Tribune, an afternoon paper, and two routes for the Tulsa World, a morning newspaper. When I started, Tom had one route and we recruited another boy to deliver the third route. During my "career," both Tom and I switched back and forth between morning and evening routes.

Routes in Broken Arrow were not like they are today. There was none of this delivering 20-30 papers in one block. Homes were scattered, and I rode my bike more than 10 miles to deliver 120 newspapers, my largest route. It was not uncommon to ride more than a half-mile to deliver to one customer. Two blocks out of downtown, paved streets became either gravel or dirt streets. We put the newspapers on the front porch.

At the end of the month, we went door to door collecting payment. For the longest time, the cost of the paper, daily and Sunday, was $1.52 a month. We got a bill from the Newspaper Printing Corp. at the end of the month for newspapers bought that month, and had about three days to make collections before the bill was due. What we had left was our profit. If everybody paid for a specific month (rare), we would make $20 to $30.

Collections were difficult, because $1.52 was a lot of money. Some customers would not have it every month. Too embarrassed to say, some would say, "Can you change a $50?" knowing that was unlikely. "Then come back next week." Others might say, "Payday is next week. Can you come back then?" There were those customers who had gardens in the backyard, or who raised a few chickens, and would want to pay the bill with potatoes, eggs or a fat hen. With these types of situations, it was difficult to pay your paper bill, much less enjoy that $30. But we managed. Each of us saved a little money each month and bought most of our own stuff, especially parts for our bikes such as tires, tubes and chains.

There was another time when carriers could make a buck or two. Whether it be county, state or federal election, candidates for office would come to town, make a pitch to prospective voters at the corner of Main and Commercial streets, and hand out handbills. "For a buck a route, we'll put your handbills in our newspapers and deliver them around town," we would say. Five bucks would get them coverage throughout the town. They couldn't beat a deal like that. With a half dozen offices up for election, and three or four candidates for each, that made pretty good money for carriers. If the newspaper management found out what we were doing, they would probably have put a stop to it. But as long as they didn't, we were always glad to see election time come around.

One day in 1947, I started my route with a slight pain in my right side. As I pedaled through the streets, the pain got worse. Finally, the pain got so bad that I went home, leaving the route for Tom to complete. Dad took one look at me and called Doc Franklin who told him to get me to the hospital and he would meet us there. That night, I was diagnosed with appendicitis and my appendix was removed. It was two weeks out of school and four weeks before I could deliver papers again. Tom was upset for having to deliver two routes, especially on the Sundays I missed. He had to double up on the chores also. One day, he would get even with me.

Dogs could be a problem to a paper boy. There were no leash laws like there are today. Everyone had a dog, some two. We got used to barking dogs and we learned to kick them away from the bike as we rode through the yard and down the street. However, one big dog knocked me off my bike and I got skinned up. From then on, I just threw his paper from the street, trying to get it as close to the porch as I could, as the dog chased me down the street. I rarely made the front porch. When I went to collect at the end of the month, the customer came to the door with 152 pennies in his hand, and said, "I'm gonna pitch these where you pitch my newspaper," and tossed them into the yard. I wasn't about to look for those pennies with that dog in the yard.

"From now on," I told him, "you can buy your paper at the drug store," and I never delivered him a paper again.

About 1949, one of the older boy's dad bought him a Cushman motor scooter. That became my ultimate desire and I wanted to dip into savings and buy one, but neither Dad nor Mom would agree to it. "Too much money," they would say, "and besides that, they are dangerous." One night, I had a dream that each of my customers gave me a dollar extra for Christmas, and that would almost be enough. That didn't happen. Then came the Whizzer motor bike, which another boy received. That was the cat's meow. Much cheaper than the Cushman, this was a reinforced bike with about a 2 HP motor forward and below the seat with a small gas tank on top. You'd pedal the bike to get the motor started and you were off.

"Don't worry Dad." I don't want a Cushman anymore. I'll settle for a Whizzer," I said. That didn't happen either.

The paper boy's worst enemy was bad weather and, of course, customers who didn't pay. Streets away from downtown would turn to mud when it rained. Navigating muddy streets in the rain was a nightmare, especially when we had to keep the newspapers dry. When it got cold and the rain turned to freezing rain, sleet, or even snow, it got worse. Then, it was most important to get a dry newspaper on the porch, where a customer could pick up the paper without getting wet.

Our newspapers were delivered to Broken Arrow by Trailways bus and dropped off at either the post office or Haskell Jones Drug store, the only bus stop in town. We folded or wrapped our papers in the alcove of a store, until the owner asked us to leave. Finally, we got some inside space at McCuistion's Pontiac dealership on North Main. The dealership was owned by the father of John Dale McCuistion, a classmate of mine. That association got us a place in the body shop, where we had to deal with the paint fumes. But, it was warm, extremely hot in the summer and dry. On the morning routes, we were stuck with a cold sidewalk storefront.

When a senior, I won a $500 scholarship from the Newspaper Printing Corp, which published both morning and evening papers. With that, working part time jobs in the summer and during semesters, war bond proceeds and the money I had saved, I went to college.

Just Sew Him Up, Doc!

Although we created our own entertainment, we weren't all that ingenious, but we had sufficient imagination to have a good time. It was the summer of 1944. Tom was 14 and Mary was almost 8, and I had just turned 10. It was one of those hot, sultry afternoons for which Oklahoma is famous. Air conditioning was natural in that it consisted of opening all the windows and hoping for a breeze. Lacking that, we would close all windows except one or two, turn on the attic fan and create a breeze through part of the house.

Our fun that afternoon was probably more of an attempt to keep cool. Barefooted and in cutoffs, (these evolved from jeans and overalls when the knees wore out--no one had a bathing suit) we played with the hose at the side of the house. Our favorite game was keep-away, and the one who had the hose had the benefit of water to assist in keeping it.

We all got our turn with the hose, but Tom, being the biggest, strongest and fastest, seemed to have it most of the time, and poor Mary rarely got it. The object was for the "have-nots" to take it away from the "have." Sometimes Mary and I collectively ganged up on Tom, and that was often successful.

We were in the side yard in an area that was much longer than the length of the hose. However, the width was only about 30 feet as we had just put in a new barbed wire pasture fence on the south side of the house. So, there was plenty of room to run, as long as you ran the right direction (east or west).

We had played for a while, but things had been pretty uneven as Tom had dominated the hose. I decided a major hell-bent onslaught would be necessary to capture the hose, so Tom and I went face to face as Mary watched. As I attacked, Tom was backing away, playing the hose in my face. I got so much water in my mouth, nose and eyes, I decided to break off the attack. As I broke off, I ran out of the force of the water, but was still unable to see. I guess I was disoriented, as I was running south, away from the house instead of east or west as I thought. I soon came to a sudden stop, tangled in barbed wire.

My chest and shoulder were all scratched up, and I had a big gash in my mouth and on my right jaw. It was back to Doc Franklin again, this time to the Broken Arrow Hospital, a new addition in town, a one story building on Main Street, just south of the elementary school. Doc Franklin was a gruff old codger who scared me. There were still lingering memories of him poking swabs down my throat to stop bleeding four years ago. His needle and thread scared me even more. But it was in a new hospital that awed me. Several stitches were required to patch me up, and I still have the scars.

After the hurt was over, and I realized it could have been much worse, an eye for example, I became proud of my wounds. I was particularly proud of the one on my jaw, because the scar nearly matched one worn by Mike. I don't remember how he got his, but it was probably a similar incident.

The accident didn't deter us from playing with the hose on those hot days. It was something to do, it kept us cool and we had fun. In the future, however, we were always more careful.

As I write these stories, it amazes me that any of us lived unscathed into adulthood. We did all these crazy things with no protection—no kneepads, no helmets, no gloves - - got banged up, then bandaged up then back to do it again. Sometimes, the cure hurt more than the injury. Stitches occasionally. That fishhook needle always hurt. Sometimes a cut was just taped shut. There was mercurochrome and iodine - - both red to orange. Mercurochrome was pleasant and iodine burned fiercely. Mom always liked to use iodine.

A Letter To Joe

During the war years, everything was sparse. There didn't seem to be much of anything except talk of this crop or that, the price of pork or beef, and war news. Communication between people seemed to occur only when they met face to face on the street in town, or at church on Sunday. Communication with relatives, 20 miles far away in Tulsa, was slim and occurred only by letter. Long distance phone calls were almost unheard of because of the expense. To call "Central" and make a long distance phone call usually meant some sort of an emergency. Three cents postage was the cost of a first class letter, and a postcard could be mailed for a penny.

Mom's older brother, Joe Eustice, lived on Reservoir Hill, in the north side of Tulsa. To us, that was the "high rent district." Big brick homes on big lots. We thought Uncle Joe was wealthy. He had a power boat on Spavinaw Lake, some 50 miles from Tulsa, and drove a big Chrysler to pull it when he wanted to go to other lakes. Joe and his wife Zeanna had nine kids. Joanne, Don, Mary Lou, Little Zeanna, Rita, Rose Marie, Larry, Eileen, and Thad made up the family. Larry was a couple of years older than I, Eileen my age and Thad a year or two younger. Their house was at the top of the hill, overlooking Tulsa. With nine kids, he needed a big house. What a beautiful view they had from a second-floor balcony. Next to their property was a higher hill that housed a Tulsa water reservoir. Mary and I looked forward to those summer days when we spent a week there, playing with our cousins on Reservoir Hill. Riding down those streets on scooters, or wagons, or even bikes was a thrill. Uncle Joe was kind of the family patriarch, two years older than a sister, Marguerite (Maggie), and four years older than Mom.

Many years later, after Mom and Maggie had died, when Uncle Joe died, a letter written to him in 1944 by Mom was recovered and returned to me. For some reason, he had kept it some 40 years. It is a reflection of earlier times and parts of it are quoted here. She must have written this letter during her lunch hour, in the shop office at the Bomber Plant where she worked, by the hunt and peck method because we had no typewriter at home.

"Bill left Saturday for the Naval Training Center at Norman and we haven't heard from him yet so don't know where he will be going next. It sure seems lonesome at home having both of the big boys gone."

Bill had graduated from high school in the Broken Arrow class of 1944, enlisted in the Navy, got through boot camp and was in a technical training course at Norman, on his way to war. Mike had finished the year before and was somewhere in the South Pacific.

"Had your letter this morning and thanks for the dollar and I was so glad to hear Don was home, if it was only for a short time."

Joe occasionally helped Mom out financially. A dollar here, a dollar there. By today's standards, this seems like such a little amount, but then, dollars were scarce and one would go a long way. Don, next to the oldest of nine kids, had been commissioned an Ensign in the Navy, and was away at war.

"Mike [my dad] has become quite an efficient housekeeper and cook and had done most of the canning so far. We have 72 pints of peas, about 40 quarts of green beans and 15 quarts of beets. We had our first potatoes out of the garden today and our first cucumber yesterday. It sure is nice to have fresh vegetables."

Since Dad was unable to work, he became the chief cook and bottle washer. He also had the farm and large garden to attend. Canning the produce of our garden was an annual ritual to feed us during the fall and winter months.

"We had a letter from Horace [brother Mike] this week, dated in May. We don't have any idea where he was, but their destination was in or close to India. He was glad to get away from their last port because the heat was

unbearable and he had been sick. He was feeling better and glad to get out to sea again and get fresh air. He hoped that his ship would go back to San Francisco after this trip."

Mike was a Navy radio operator assigned to the armed guard on a merchant ship that hauled needed war supplies and freight back and forth between Southeast Asia and the U.S. One trip would be guns, the next trucks. The last one was mules. It was a "Mister Roberts" type of ship. We never knew where he was in the South Pacific. There was much censorship of the mail because of military secrecy, and a letter seemed forever in transit.

"The kids are out of school and lots of help around home and in the garden."

We all had chores to do when we were at home. Harvesting the large garden, including weeding, shelling, husking, and canning was always a family operation, on top of feeding animals, gathering eggs, and milking cows.

"John had a slight accident last week while playing in the water with the hose. He ran into the barbed wire fence and looked like he ran into a buzz saw. He had a long scratch on his shoulder, a cut on his lip and cheek. Mike took him to the Dr. and he took stitches in his lip and cheek and gave him a tetnus shot. Never a dull moment at the Connerys."

With three small kids at home, there was always something.

"I talked to Meg [her sister] *a few days ago and she hadn't heard from Pat* [her son] *for over two weeks so suppose he is on the way across* [to the European theater] *by now. I will sure be glad when this horrible nightmare is over and people can return to a more settled life."*

These were the thoughts of all of us back home. It was just a few weeks later that Pat, Meg's youngest son, was killed during the Battle of the Bulge, a famous WWII battle between the U.S. and Germany in Belgium. He was awarded the Silver Star for his actions. He was buried in a temporary military cemetery and his body was returned home after the war. I was 12 at the time and served as an altar boy at his funeral mass. Her oldest, Clifford (Hank) was somewhere in Europe.

"Hope you have a nice birthday and wish I could help you celebrate. It doesn't seem possible you will be 45. You know I sure would like to go to a

good dance sometime. Why don't we do that? I'll admit I am getting pretty old for such foolishness but it has been so long I would just like to go to a dance like I used to. Of course I don't know who I would go with or what I would wear and dear me I never did get my permanent. Oh well, I can dream can't I? No fools no fun."

The first time I read this, it brought a tear to my eye. It was the first time I thought of my mom as being a young woman, rather than just Mom. She was just 40, and for the past seven years, her husband had been an invalid, an invalid who devoted all of his energies to running a farm and a household. No more moving bales of hay around and hosting dances in the barn loft. No more going out with friends on the weekend. Rarely did they play bridge anymore. Not much more fun in married life. Continual worry about Dad's health, safety of two sons off to fight a war, while keeping food on the table for the remaining three.

"Sometimes it doesn't seem so long since we were kids going to school and do you remember how we used to fuss about who was going to carry the lunch bucket and how we used to stop in at that bakery on Third Street and get some cinnamon rolls for our lunch and how good we thought they were?"

This generation remembered the good ol' days.

Bathroom Doors

Our home started as a very small farmhouse in 1924 and was expanded as necessary as the family grew. Originally, Dad built a small one-bedroom house, with living room and combined kitchen-dining room. The toilet was in the backyard. A small basement/storm cellar was underneath. When Mike and Bill came along, the first expansion included another bedroom and bathroom facilities inside. Our house was of hodge-podge construction.

Construction began again in 1934 when I was born, leaving us with three bedrooms, living room, entry room, kitchen/dining room, an enclosed back porch and a bathroom. The entry room (I call it that for lack of a better name) was where the front door was, and it also doubled as my bedroom until Tom went to college. So, when someone came in the front door, they also came through my bedroom. Because of the way the house was constructed piecemeal, our bathroom had three doors-- one from the back bedroom (Dad's), one on the opposite wall from the enclosed back porch, and one from the living room.

It was awfully hard for anybody to get any privacy in the bathroom. None of the doors had locks, and invariably someone would enter during a private moment. It always seemed safer to go outside to a tree. I'm sure Mary didn't think that way, however. But, there were seven of us sharing that bathroom and three doors. Saturday night was bath night (no shower), making the bathroom like Grand Central Station. With three younger kids in the house, the first one to bathe got the clean water.

The door from the living room caused embarrassment in three ways.

It was embarrassing to have company come into the house with that door standing open. It was especially embarrassing to be sitting on the commode when someone opened that door with company in the living room. The least embarrassment was when you had company, had to excuse yourself, and walk directly into the bathroom. I don't think it bothered us kids that much--especially in our younger years, but I know that it must have been embarrassing to Mom and Dad on occasion. In any event, embarrassment aside, the traffic control problem through the bathroom had to be akin to the one at O'Hare International Airport.

The neat thing about the living room entrance was its closeness. It wasn't bad at all, waking up in the middle of the night in my bedroom (the entry room), walking up two steps into the living room, and straight across to the bathroom door. (Now that I write this, I realize I had a sunken bedroom--the living room was raised).

Then one day, Dad decided we didn't need that door. Two would be enough. Perhaps he wanted to eliminate some of the embarrassing situations; or maybe he thought "uptown" people just don't have a door to the bathroom from the living room. Whatever, the reason, he closed down that door, walled it off, and the couch was placed along that wall.

That really took some getting used to, especially at night. I can't remember the number of times I crawled out of bed in the middle of the night, ran up those steps, across the living room, and smack dab into a couch and wall--ending in a sudden stop. It was enough to wake everyone. Others in the family did the same thing at one time or another.

The path was to go through Mom's bedroom and on through Dad's bedroom, and into the bathroom. We could not use this way at night, but instead would go through the kitchen onto be enclosed porch (not heated in winter) and into the bathroom, or go outside. There were plenty of trees either in front or back to pee on. Somehow, this often seemed the easiest. Once in the bathroom, however, one had only to worry about two doors, neither of which had a lock.

Home Entertainment

Kids come home today and they watch their choice of about 200 channels on cable TV; or they play video games on their cell phone, X-Box or I-pad or they turn on NETFLIX or put a CD they just picked up at the 7-11 into the DVR and watch a movie; and they wonder what they would do---how they would survive without it. The modern family has the "home entertainment center," which consists of everything. But before that, Mom makes them do their homework so they open their ipad, get on the internet and read a homework assignment.

It wasn't that way in our day. When it came to homework, it was to read a chapter and answer questions; do 20 math problems, or perhaps write a theme about something.

We didn't even have a vehicle with a radio. We didn't have a vehicle. We had only one radio--in the living room, and that was it. It was the kind of radio you see in flea markets or antique shows today--the one which stood tall, was rounded on the top, had a little bitty dial, a lot of vacuum tubes in back, and had a logo on front of a dog listening to an old speaker.

With this state of the art equipment, we could get two, perhaps three radio stations in Tulsa, all AM. FM radio was still on the drawing board. Sirius was someone's dream. There were no talk shows. and the only music show was the Hit Parade on Saturday night with Snooky Lansing and Dorothy Collins; or we could hear live country and western music from Leon McAulliffe or Johnny Lee Wells at noon, Monday through Saturday.

I'm sure, with seven people in the house, we had arguments

concerning what we would listen to, just like those that occur today in front of the TV. Dad or Mom always settled those arguments promptly. The evening entertainment, after homework, was gathering around that magic box, listening to the words that came out of it, and turning your imagination loose to picture in your mind what they looked like, the type of clothes they wore, and the type of cars that were above the screech of the wheels. Radio was truly the "theatre of the mind," as it has been defined.

The programming was good quality. If you ever hear an old time celebrity being interviewed about which is hardest, radio or TV, you'll hear him say, 9 times out of 10 that radio was the hardest. Not only did he have to get the words across, but he had to create an illusion--a picture in your mind as to what was going on. Even though Tom, Mary and I all heard the same words and sound effects, I'd bet we all saw different pictures racing across our minds. For an excellent example of this, listen to Orson Wells' "War of the Worlds," which usually is broadcast (on radio) each year at Halloween. During that original broadcast in the late 1930s, people missed the announcement that it was just fiction, and pandemonium resulted in eastern cities, causing car wrecks, suicides, and the like. We were being taken over.

There was "Fibber McGee and Molly," and the noise of things tumbling out of the hall closet when he opened the door; there was the squeaking door of "Inner Sanctum," and the fear created with wondering what would be behind the door tonight; the stern voice of "Mr. District Attorney," as he put bad guys in the slammer; the slapstick comedy of black comedians "Amos and Andy"; and the nickel/dime betting among ourselves as to what would be at the top of the Saturday night "Hit Parade." Later on Saturday night, Dad would listen to the fights. I remember closing my eyes and seeing Joe Louis pound an opponent. In retrospect, I prefer that to television. You are forced to use your imagination to complete the picture. TV does it all and makes one lazy.

As Mike and Bill got older, they had a record player in their bedroom that played the old 78s. I remember when they would have friends out and listen and dance to records playing music by Tommy Dorsey, Benny

Goodman, Glen Miller and Harry James. On vocals by groups like the Andrews Sisters, they would listen over and over, writing down the words to the songs so they could sing along.

When I joined the Cub Scouts, one of my first projects was to make flower bouquet holders for Mom for Mother's Day. "Take an old 78 RPM record and put it in a pan of water," the leader said as she carefully lit the stove burner beneath the water pan. "Heat the water to a boil then turn the burner off." The record could then be curled from the sides and molded into a nice flower holder. I made several of these before I got one right. The older brothers were gone and wouldn't need them. Mom liked the one I gave her and actually put flowers in it, but she let me know I would be in trouble when they came home. This was one of their favorite records.

We all learned to play a number of card games. Cribbage and gin rummy were popular. We developed our own versions of double solitaire. Canasta came along and we learned that. Mom and Dad liked to play bridge and most of us were taught that. One Christmas, there was a family gift of Monopoly. It didn't take long before each of us wanted to own Park Avenue.

In years before I can remember, Mom and Dad would have barn dances in the hay barn. Bales of hay would be cleared to the side, leaving a slick, wooden floor. A fiddle player, guitarist and a drummer at one end could have friends dancing till the wee hours of the morning. A bale of hay was comfortable to sit on and Mary and I were small enough to lie down on when sleep caught up with us.

A follow-up chapter sets the stage for TV coming to Broken Arrow for the first time. The change had started. In most ways, the change has been for the good, but in some ways, I'd rather return to the ways of the radio and the fiddle player in the barn.

An Unscheduled Afternoon At Bob's

Bundles of the Tulsa Tribune were late arriving in Broken Arrow that day. The newspapers were in bundles of 50. I took three bundles, and had two or three copies of the newspaper left when I finished my route. Tom took about the same amount and delivered to stores along Main Street before going into his neighborhood. I folded mine, bagged them, then headed out on my bike to deliver the west side of town. They came by Trailways bus, and it had broken down somewhere between Broken Arrow and Tulsa.

I was there--ready to pick them up and get finished. There would be a good sandlot football game at Jack Hudson's later that afternoon, and I wanted to get finished and go play. Sometimes, I stopped in the middle of my route for this type of activity, and many customers got their paper late, often about dark. I had an at least an hour to kill before the bus would arrive. It was too early to go to Jack's. There wasn't enough time to go home and come back. And I couldn't sit in the drug store for an hour as I didn't have any money, and would just be taking up room.

I went to Bob Arnold's house. Bob lived just off Main Street, about three blocks away. He was in my fifth grade class, and was a good friend of mine. We spent a lot of time together doing the kinds of things 11-year-old boys do.

Bob was about my build, wore glasses and had bright red hair, and we liked to do the same kind of things. I didn't know it at the time, but Bob, whose Dad worked in the coal mines, would move the next year, and I wouldn't see him again. I got preoccupied playing at Bob's, and one and one-half hours had gone by before I realized it. I had to go and take care of my route.

I rode my bike north on his street to Dallas, where I had to turn right. There was a stop sign, but I went around that stop the same way I see adults doing it today. I found myself face to face with an old Ford pickup coming toward me on the wrong side of the street. I put the bike into a skid, and his left front tire ran over my bike, and the left front fender knocked me about 15 feet into the street. I laid there in the street---bruised, skinned up, bleeding, and hurting. I could not move.

I spent a day or two in the hospital and after they found I had no broken bones or internal injuries, they sent me home. I laid in bed for almost a week, hurting too much to walk. Tom came to my rescue and delivered my route as well as his for a week. It was good to get back to my route, but was sure slow going for awhile.

My Dad was angry--not at me for a change. He was angry with the fellow who was on the wrong side of the street and ran over me. Gene Flowers, Chief of Police (the total police force) had cited the other driver accordingly. My Dad was so angry that I got a completely rebuilt bike out of it. It was in much better shape than before it was wrecked. Dad used a different kind of an approach. I had technically run the stop sign, and that was the driver's defense. Dad said, "If I even thought, for a moment, that you went onto the wrong side of the street just to run over this kid because he ran a stop sign, I'd get my shotgun and shoot you." This was effective negotiating. I know that at other times Dad went to bat for me, but I remember this time most of all.

I've always blamed Trailways for the accident. If the bus would have been on time, I would have never been at Bob's, and the accident would not have happened.

A Week In Tulsa

We never took a vacation as a family. I suppose there were many reasons for not doing so, including economic, Dad's health, no car; and besides that, somebody always had to be around to milk the cows, tend the garden, and feed the livestock. Family vacations were completely foreign to me, and continued to be through my adult life. Vacations during my Navy career occurred every two or three years, and consisted of the move we made with each duty station transfer, which usually included a trip back to Oklahoma. Even then, we never stopped to smell the roses.

Mary and I always got a week off during the summer. We would get to spend a week in Tulsa, with Uncle Horace and Aunt Rose Wilson (Dad's sister) or Uncle Joe and Aunt Zeanna Eustice (Mom's brother). Tom, a little older, and because of his interest in livestock, would spend a week in Pawhuska on the ranch with Uncle Will and Aunt Mary Higgins (Dad's sister). I always wanted to go up there for a week, but never got the chance.

Tulsa was fun--it was the big city. All sorts of things to do and see that we never had in Broken Arrow. The Wilson and Eustice homes were quite different from one another, so both visits were completely different. Mary and I usually went together, and some years we would get to go both places in the same summer.

Uncle Horace and Aunt Rose had two daughters, twins Ruth and Claire. They were Tom's age, so in most cases, Mary and I were pests to them. Aunt Rose would take charge of entertaining us. She would take us across town on a city bus to Newblock swimming pool, a public park area. That was the first real pool I was ever in, and boy, was that uptown, especially when combined with the bus ride. After that, we came back to Broken Arrow and really impressed our friends.

I remember two other things about visits to Aunt Rose. Two blocks away, there was a Hires Root Beer Stand. The treat of the day--if we were good--was a walk to Hires for a root beer float. How good that tasted on a hot summer day. Things just couldn't get much better than that.

One time, I got me in trouble with Uncle Horace. They had a small garage which just barely housed their Pontiac. When he came home from work and put the car in the garage, I would sit behind the wheel and play like I was driving. Remember Arney? I took him with me for a drive around the block. That was a thrill because there was no car at home to play in. Invariably, I played the role of a race car driver, speeding rapidly down the track and making those sharp turns. One time, I left the wheels turned about 45 degrees. When Uncle Horace backed out to go to work next morning, he thought the wheels were straight. He put a big dent in a front fender backing out and almost took the side of the garage out. I didn't get to play in the car again.

Vacations at the home of Uncle Joe and Aunt Zeanna were quite different. Lots of kids. Joe and Zeanna had nine, about six of whom were home. They lived on Reservoir Hill in North Tulsa in a big two-story brick house. Right next to them was the Tulsa water reservoir, which was even higher. There was a commanding view of downtown Tulsa. The streets were all narrow, residential, and curved around the hill, up and down. They were fantastic for riding down on bikes or scooters. Coming back up the hill was slower and harder, but well worth the thrill going down. At the end of the week, we went home with skinned knees, shins, and bruises, caused from failing to make one of the curves. We never wore helmets or protective clothing, so it is a wonder we never had a serious accident. Just two blocks to the east of the house was what I remember as being a big cliff--it wasn't really that big, but from a little boy's perspective, it was gigantic. There was a little cave in the side, and cousins Larry, Thad and I would make a fortress and fight the bad guys.

Occasionally, we--if we were good--(we always had to be good), would get a treat there also. Uncle Joe was a member of the Tulsa Country Club--which had its origins in the oil boom, long before Southern Hills. That's where the elite went. At least once and perhaps twice during the week, we went to the club and swam. That was private--not public like Newblock. We had stories to tell when we got home. Tom came home from the ranch telling stories about riding horses and roping calves. It was always fun to exchange stories.

Although we never had a family vacation, we kids usually had ours. The memories of a little country boy going to the big city are still vivid in my mind and were an important part of my growing up. In those years when we didn't get that Tulsa trip, there were always ways to daydream.

That picture and a good imagination made many good "vacations" for this young boy.

Fourth Of July

The Fourth of July was always the big family get-together at my house. We never had this sort of thing at Christmas, Thanksgiving or New Year's. Those were days for individual families to gather and celebrate.

Why was the Fourth such a big family celebration? Perhaps because it was patriotic, and a reminder from WWII. Perhaps it was because we could all gather and celebrate the freedom we had, and agree on what that freedom meant to us. Perhaps it was because Dad was a WWI veteran who saw, during that war, the lack of freedom in Germany and France. Perhaps it was because of World War II. Or maybe it was the middle of a hot summer, and we needed the opportunity to gather, socialize, celebrate, and forget the heat for awhile. The reason is unimportant. What is important is that it was a fixture in our family, and everyone started looking forward to it about the first of June. It all started in Broken Arrow at my parents' home.

It must have been nice for all those city relatives to be able to tell their friends they were going to the country to celebrate the Fourth. And it was always nice for us to have the city folk come grace our home. After each Fourth was over, we would get a big write up in the Broken Arrow Ledger about the folks who came all the way from Tulsa to celebrate with us. You could expect to see a large cast of characters on the Fourth. Dad had five sisters who lived in the Tulsa area. Aunt Rose and Uncle Horace Wilson lived in Tulsa and had twin daughters, Ruth and Claire, who were Tom's age. Aunt Claire and Uncle Walter McAuley, also from Tulsa, had daughters Ruth, Tom's age, and Ellen, between Tom and me. Aunt Mary and Uncle Will Higgins were ranch people from Pawhuska. There were also Aunt Ruth and Aunt Elizabeth, Dad's sisters who never married.

On Mom's side, there was a brother, Uncle Joe and Aunt Zeanna, and some of their nine kids, from the big house on reservoir hill in Tulsa. Larry, Eileen and Thad in that family were my running mates. Mom's sister was Marguerite Southwood, and she was married to Uncle Newt, and they had two boys, Clifford (Hank) and Pat, who were both in Mike and Bill's age group. Along with them were always Doc Jones, an Irish osteopath, and his girlfriend Mildred.

I don't remember any one Fourth when all of the above came at the same time. But at one time or another, they were all there. Family and friends gathered with neighbors to celebrate with us.

Preparation for the Fourth was always a big evolution. Days previous were spent mowing the yard, trimming around the fence and trees, whitewashing the trees, and cleaning the house. Harvesting the garden, shucking corn, snapping beans and shelling peas were always an all hands task. A couple of days before, we killed and cleaned chickens. The milk that made the ice cream spent last night in the cow, and most everybody got a turn cranking the freezer.

I remember that a week to 10 days before, Tom and I, with Dad's help (it was really just Tom, but I like to think I helped) operated a fireworks stand in the front yard, and what was left over, we shot the night of the Fourth. The road in front of our house was the city limits line, and often, Chief of Police Gene Flowers tried to shut us down, but Dad told him in no uncertain terms where he could go.

They all came on the Fourth--at least most of them. They brought friends and relatives, and we invited friends. Some brought food, dessert, and all brought fireworks. It was the kind of Fourth of July celebration that you see occasionally in the movies, or read about in a book--the good, old-fashioned kind.

On one Fourth, the county was re-surfacing Lynn Lane Road in front of the house. We were finally getting a black top road. The county had graded, and regraded, mixing the gravel, dirt and black top material, and left it piled in a long ribbon, two feet wide, 14 inches high, in the middle of the road. At intervals along the road, there were breaks in the ribbon where a vehicle could cross from one side to the other. In the days following graders would spread the ribbon and pack it down. Doc Jones, Mildred, Newt and Maggie got to our driveway and found they were on the wrong side of the ribbon. Their choice was to cross it or go down the road a half mile and get on the other side. Doc and Newt had been nipping on the sauce on the way out, and they decided they could cross it. Their car ended up high and dry on top of the ribbon, blocking both the north and south lanes. We had to dig them out.

The menu was great. Fried chicken, potato salad, baked beans, corn on the cob, and lots of fresh vegetables from the garden were savored prior to homemade ice cream and pies and cakes.

When it got dark, we kids, with adult supervision, went into the front yard to shoot fireworks. One time, a sky rocket, or something similar, started a fire on the football field across the road. One year, from the fireworks stand, we saved a rocket type of firework that sent a little man down in a parachute. We had three of them, and I wanted to keep that man and parachute. On the first one, the parachute burned, the second came down somewhere else, and the third was the only one salvaged. "I want it," I cried, as I ran toward the little man floating down in the parachute.

My cousin Ellen McAuley got there first and picked it up from the grass. "I've got it - - I want it!" she exclaimed. It caused a big flap, but Mom told me to let her have it, because she was company. It really upset me that I didn't get to keep it.

Someone always managed to get burned, usually from a sparkler, or a fire cracker going off in someone's hand, but a little butter and TLC always seemed to soothe the wounds.

One of the most memorable Fourths was in 1946 when I was 12. The war was over and the boys were home, or soon would be, from the war. It was truly a time to celebrate. We had gone through all the preparations previously described. Everything was ready for company and the big celebration. The smells from the kitchen were delicious. The yard was spic and span, the trees were whitewashed, and the ice cream mix was chilling and ready to freeze. It was time for guests to start arriving. Most of the crowd would be coming that year.

Catastrophe!! Mom discovered that she forgot to get napkins. That couldn't be. We had to have them. We couldn't expect guests to eat fried chicken and corn on the cob without napkins. So I went to town on my bike, 3/4 miles away, to get them. I would save the day. The only store open on the Fourth in Broken Arrow was Haskell Jones drug store. I knew Haskell, and he knew me. He was one of my newspaper customers. I walked into the store and told Haskell I needed some napkins. When he asked, "Do you want the sanitary kind?" I was insulted. I thought he may be implying that we might not be sanitary in the way we lived.

"Hell yes," I replied, trying to be authoritative. "We're as sanitary as any of you folk who live in town."

"How many do you want?"

"I need a lot. Just put them on the tab. We have a lot of company coming."

So, I walked out and stuffed two giant sized boxes into my bike basket. I did not understand why boxes of napkins were wrapped in brown paper. I just wasn't in the know. I was proud of myself. I had done the job necessary to bail Mom out of a predicament. She would be happy.

I rode into the driveway and back yard after some guests had already arrived. Fortunately, I had made it back before anyone had started eating. I made a big presentation of two boxes of Kotex wrapped in brown paper to Mom in the back yard, in front of company.

For a long time, I didn't understand why I was not appreciated. I had gone and got what she needed--even the sanitary kind. As I've looked back at this over the years, I should be glad that the boxes were wrapped in plain brown paper. That probably saved some embarrassment. I would bet that Haskell Jones knew what I really wanted and substituted the "sanitary kind," then laughed as he would tell that story to friends until a better one came along.

When we finally sat down to eat that day, there were napkins on the table. I have no idea where they came from.

Going To The Dentist

Our dentist, during those early years, was our next door neighbor. He was a gentleman dairy farmer, a dentist, and a deacon in the Assembly of God Church. He had two sons, Max, who grew up and graduated with Tom, and Gene, a year younger than me.

Dr. Brissey was the only dentist in town for a number of years. He had the market locked in. He practiced dentistry for many years. Years later, I drove through Broken Arrow and saw the sign: "Dr. C.C. Brissey, DDS; Practice of Dentistry." He was still drilling, filling and billing, and he must have been in his 70s. Dr. Brissey died as the first draft of this book was written. He had been a fixture in the Broken Arrow I grew up in for a number of years.

Dr. Brissey was an Elder, or Deacon, or perhaps both, in the Assembly of God Church. We Catholics knew that those non-Catholics didn't have much of a chance; and Doc Brissey knew that if we weren't "saved," we wouldn't make it either. I guess an outsider would conclude that it was a Mexican standoff and that none of us would make it, but we would meet someplace.

Doc Brissey had a captive audience when he got one of us in his chair, and his drill in the mouth. Not only did we have the normal fear of going to the dentist, we went knowing that we could come away with chinks drilled out of our faith.

Doc Brissey had a frightening looking drilling rig. It consisted of two or three long arms connected by swivel joints, hinges, pulleys, belts and a slow motor. At the end of it was the drill. This is not to say that Doc had ancient equipment. It was probably state of the art. The high-speed air drill that is common today didn't exist then, at least in Broken Arrow.

Doc always had music in his office--at least when we were there. It was not the elevator music you hear today, and I am sure Muzak wouldn't place it in a department store. We heard Assembly of God Music: Hymns, hallelujahs, and Praise the Lord. Doc would get that drill down into a nerve ending during that moment between hymns, be grinding away, and he would start to preach. At that point in time, you'd listen to anything to get that drill out of your mouth.

While drilling, he would hum along with the music, and preach a little too--an occasional "Praise the Lord," or something similar. Now that I think about it, I wonder why mom would not let me be a shepherd in the School Christmas Play held at the Baptist Church; yet would send me to Doc Brissey.

Then one day, Dr. Sylvester E. Spann came to town and set up practice. He was a fantastic dentist--a commander in the Naval Reserve--which got him some points with us--and he didn't preach. From then on, he took care of our teeth.

I was kind of a snaggle-tooth kid. Doc Spann told Mom that they could be straightened with something called braces. He explained the process to us, the time required, and all the metal that would be in my mouth.

"How much will this cost," Mom asked, not really convinced this was needed.

"About five hundred," I think he replied.

Mom could not stop laughing. That was so far out of sight for us. We just didn't have that kind of money. Just a few years later, I got hit across the mouth by an elbow block from Glenn Cone in a football scrimmage that deadened my four front teeth. That solved the problem, as the day before high school graduation, these four teeth were pulled and a partial denture installed.

Milk Cream And Butter

Until Tom started to college in 1948, we always milked cows. I suppose, at one time, we may have milked as many as 10. I don't recall, during my early years, that we sold milk. I know that in years previous, Dad developed a milk and egg route, but that was in the early 1930s.

We had a cream separator on the back porch. What we didn't need as whole milk was put in a large container at the top of this device. This usually amounted to 3 4 gallons unless one of the cows stepped in the milk bucket, which occurred once in a while. An operating handle is manually turned, spinning an arrangement of conical-shaped discs at a high rate of speed. As the milk runs through these discs, centrifugal force separates the cream from the milk into separate containers. I turned that handle every day for what seemed like years. I've always liked cold milk, but the best milk ever was that which was warm, and fresh from the cow.

After cream separation, the resulting milk was about 1% fat, and did not taste very good. We fed it to the pigs. Now, it's the only milk I will drink because whole milk is just too heavy. This probably has something to do with growing older.

The cream was extremely rich, and we used it in coffee, on cereal, and on desserts like strawberry shortcake. Occasionally, we would splurge, and make homemade ice cream. We would save what we didn't use for the above purposes, and when we had enough, we'd take it to the basement and make butter.

Dad had rigged a butter churn that consisted of a square can holding about 2 gallons, and a paddle-type dasher that was turned by a small electric motor. When the butter was made, into a big wooden dish it would go to be salted, worked over with a spatula, and placed in a mold that formed one-pound blocks. That's what we put on the table, and it was good. There was nothing better than a glob of that on a thick slice of freshly baked, freshly sliced homemade bread. What was left over after the butter was buttermilk. We would chill it and drink it, or Dad would use it to make biscuits.

Sometimes, Mom put whole milk it in a large bowl, cover it with a towel, and put it in a low-temperature oven. The milk would sour, and thicken into a curdle called clabber. From that, she would make cottage cheese, and something like yogurt.

I became quite attached to that cream separator. I always marveled at how it worked--it was an engineering masterpiece. The only bad thing about it was cleaning it after each use. All of those discs had to be taken apart and washed individually, then reassembled for use after the next milking.

Watermelon

As a kid, it was always fun to ice down a watermelon on a hot Sunday, cut and eat it, then spit seeds at one another. Sometimes, we dried the seeds and planted them. When we bought one from a stand, we took it to the old ice house in Broken Arrow and had it chilled.

Another thing fun about watermelons was stealing them from a farmer's patch. That could often be dangerous, but it always created a sense of excitement. I couldn't help but think of "Buck" Ragsdale when going out on one of these missions. I did this only a few times, but there was one time I remember well.

Herman Ragsdale was the football coach at Broken Arrow High. He was a great coach, with several conference championships over the years. In his later years, he retired from coaching and became high school principal. In the early 1930s, his high school days, he was a running back for Broken Arrow. But he had a dark side too. While a running back, legend has it, he was caught stealing a watermelon, and shot from a distance by an irate farmer with a shotgun. Somehow, he got back into town and was laid out on a pool table in the local bar while the buckshot was removed from his back, legs and buttocks. Thus, the name "Buck," which he carried the rest of his life. That name was reserved for only his closest friends. For a student to call him that was double trouble.

Tom and I had finished our paper routes and were home. It was still too early to start the evening chores, and we were looking for something to do. Tom said, "Let's go get a watermelon." The summer heat made that seem like a good idea. It did not occur to me that we weren't going to town to buy one.

We got on our bikes and took off. Instead of turning right onto Dallas to go into town, we headed south along Lynn Lane road about two miles to a farm where there was a big watermelon patch. "We'll get one here," Tom said. The thought of getting one right out of the field got my adrenalin pumping.

He left me at the fence to stand guard, and he climbed through, and disappeared into the patch as I watched up and down the road for cars. Soon, he was back with a big melon and set it in my basket. I was on my bike and ready to leave, when he said, "Wait a minute--we've got to pay for this and I don't have any money."

"How much?" I asked.

"Fifty cents" was the reply. I had collected from a couple of customers that day so I had some change in my pocket. I found a half dollar and gave it to him.

"How do we pay him?" I asked.

"Dummy, we leave it on a leaf of the plant where I took it." Knowing that he was older and wiser than I (I was continually reminded), I accepted him at face value. "The farmer will get it when he makes his rounds in the morning." He again disappeared through the fence with my money in his hand. I resigned myself to the obvious fact that it was my treat today. Soon, he was back and we got on our bikes and went home. We cooled the melon in water and ate it that evening.

The excitement of stealing a watermelon was fun; yet I felt no guilt because I had "paid" for it. I didn't even mention it the next Sunday when I went to Confession.

Then one day--whether a week, month, or year later (I don't know how long)--I thought about the watermelon caper. I was then a little older and wiser, and I realized Tom had conned me out of fifty cents. There was just no way he had left that money in the field. He put it in his pocket. Tom had gotten the best of me again.

Tom conned me on other occasions. I guess that's what big brothers are for. It helps you grow up faster. Each time was a learning experience, and at least, this time, we kept the money in the family.

Headed To Camp

It was the spring of 1946 and I was nearing the age of 12. Boy Scout camp was on the horizon and I was excited. I didn't know much about camp but I was looking forward to going. I had finished three years as a Cub Scout. I had attended weekly meetings for three years at Bill Baker's house (his Mom was the Den Mother), always wearing that uniform with neckerchief, long stockings and knicker pants. That's where I learned how to make bouquet holders out of 78 RPM phonograph records.

There were two troops in Broken Arrow, 103 and 104. Tom had belonged to Troop 103 with his best friend Bob Henry. Most troops today are sponsored by churches. Not then, at least not in Broken Arrow. If there was sponsorship, it was by the business owned by the leader - - Troop 103 by a dry cleaners and 104 by a barber shop. Troop 103 had been a good group and had once been the best choice. Now, Troop 104 had become the most popular among my peers and they would be going to camp first so that's the one I joined. We would be off to Camp Garland for a week the week after my 12th birthday.

I didn't know that tents were provided and I had saved my nickels and dimes during the winter to buy a tent. One morning, on the back of a cereal box was an ad for a 1-man tent that was waterproof with a self contained floor, air vents, mosquito netting and a zippered-flap for security. It could be set up and taken down in 10 minutes. It was just what I wanted - - the cat's meow, we would say and was not expensive. I could afford it. It would only take six box tops and $5.99. We had to eat a lot of that cereal to get the box tops. It would cut down on the times Dad would have to make Malt-O-Meal, a hot cereal that none of us liked. I encouraged Mary and Tom to eat a bowl every morning until it was gone. Tom helped but Mary didn't like it, so was not much help. We finally emptied the last box and I put the tops together and mailed them with a money order I had purchased at the post office. For two weeks, I anxiously awaited arrival of my tent, checking with the post office daily. Finally, it arrived and I quickly set it up in the front yard. It looked magnificent, truly the cat's meow. I slept in it that night and was not bothered by mosquitoes, bears or other animals, and kept dry in the early morning rain. It was compact, light, and would fit into a knapsack that I would wear on my back. I was ready for camp.

There were perhaps a half-dozen new scouts and 10-12 older boys who went to camp that week, accompanied by two or three adults. We arrived on Sunday afternoon and spent the rest of the day setting up camp. I remember the names of most, but will not identify them. All except me lived/slept in 4-man tents. Here was me, in my little 1-man tent, at the end of the row. Who would you think got picked on? It was not uncommon to find the stakes pulled out of my tent and it collapsed on the ground. That was a popular sport, and it happened to me late one night with me in it. I was to be the camp scapegoat for the week.

This type of treatment carried over to camp activities, like putting a worm in my tray at dinner and sabotaging my merit badge work. I learned to hunt snipe the first night, and the leader was very surprised I caught one. We swam every day, but we had to pass a 50-yard swim test to get into deep water. The camp was on a finger of Grand Lake O' the Cherokees in northeastern Oklahoma. The finger was divided into two areas - - one for beginners and another for those who had passed the 50-yard swim test. We swam on a buddy system and if we were caught without our buddy, we had to sit out. Frequently, my buddy would disappear and I would be in trouble. I was not a strong swimmer, and it took me until Thursday to pass the test so I could swim and play water games with the rest of the troop.

One day that week, we were sent out to pick up firewood for the big bonfire. I got lost. But I found a big piece of firewood, lying in the brush. I struggled for what seemed like hours to bring it back to camp.

It probably wouldn't have taken so long if I had known where camp was. What I drug back that evening was part of a Cherokee Indian totem pole, which through rot, ants, and wind, had fallen down in a sacred Indian burial ground. It had once been a landmark at Camp Garland. I struggled and struggled to get this piece of firewood back to camp. I was proud of myself, and thought perhaps I would regain some of the stature lost because of the tent. The Scoutmaster looked at me--then at the pole--then back again at me--and I knew I was in trouble. I was told there would be a meeting of the camp council that night to decide whether I should be sent home or not. Something about desecration of Indian Grounds. The Cherokees might go to war. They told me that I would be haunted by Cherokee Ghosts, which kept me awake that night. But, I was allowed to stay. Because I had been lost, because of the tent, and because of the totem pole, Jim Hocker, another scout, nicknamed me Daniel Boone that night. When I graduated from high school six years later, many of my classmates still called me Daniel.

Friday night, the last night in camp, things got bad. This manuscript was written some 30 years ago without this part. Now, writing it for publication, I have included it after much thought. My wife, as my first editor, has heard this story for the first time. I have discussed it with my pastor and a retired scout leader who has devoted 50 years to scouting. They have both been very encouraging. My final editor commends me for the courage it takes to tell this story.

While the adults were off doing something else, the ringleader of some older scouts collected another boy and me, took us to the back side of the camp for our final initiation, made us sit down side by side, take off our pants, and masturbate each other while the other boys watched. Then, I wouldn't have known what that word meant. "Jack him off—jackim, jackim!" some of the other boys shouted.

We were so frightened. I remember it so well. I had somehow bruised my left hand so he reversed our positions so I could use my right. He thought that was funny. I wanted to scream for help, but it would have done no good. We were at his mercy.

Afterward, I wanted to tell the leader, but did not know what to tell him. When I came home, I didn't know how to tell my parents, I wanted to tell my brother Tom, but could not. I remember wondering if this is what scouting was all about. The other boy and I grew up together but never talked about it. Later, I played in the band with the older boy until he graduated and was gone. I wanted to say something to him, wanted to hit him, wanted to tell on him, but for some reason, couldn't. I guess I was afraid of him. I did not know how. I just know that I never liked him. At this writing, I have found his address, written and forgiven him.

I think this has screwed up my life. I am 83 years old now, and my life could have been so much better if this had never happened. Maybe a clinical psychologist could explain all of the sexual hang-ups I have had during my life. I have never had any counseling, but instead have kept this inward all my life. Now, you, the reader, know. I regret that I was never able to tell my dad.

I had paid my dues.

In spite of all these problems, I went back to scout camp at least two more times, hoping to find better memories. The next time, my Dad went as a counselor--because at the last minute, one cancelled out and we needed one or the trip would be cancelled, Dad volunteered. That's about the only thing I ever remember my Dad doing with me, except occasional fishing on a Saturday afternoon. That experience had its bad times too--the thinking at the time--you can't have any real fun when Dad's there-- was not without merit, but I was really glad he went. Dad did most of the cooking, and we really ate well.

I bear no ill feelings toward the boy scouts, just a bad memory. I have two nephews who are Eagle Scouts, and each has a son who is an Eagle and I am extremely proud of them. However, I think this is a story that has to be told, and is just an example of unsupervised "boys being boys." It is a story that, for my own reasons, has never been told until now. I was 15 the last year I went to camp. There was a skit night that year around a bonfire the last night of camp. All troops in camp had to do something. Some of us played in the high school band and we brought our instruments. We combined our music with a skit. It was a super production and there was no question about who had the best show. We probably really weren't that good, but we were better than anyone else.

In retrospect, my scout camp experience was fun. But as you can see, there was a lot of pain. Pain, that was with me, one way or another, through my adult years. If I were to do it again, I would go without the pain.

John Rodgers' Farm

John Rodgers was the only other person in my class who was Catholic. We had different backgrounds, although in a lot of ways, they were similar. Through that bond of religion, we became very good friends. John lived on a farm--much bigger than ours.

Although I saw John every day at school, the thing I looked forward to was seeing him at church on Sunday. We often were altar boys together and that enhanced that bond. The thing I looked forward to was an invitation to go home with him after church.

John had a brother and sister who were grown and gone. I never got to meet them. There were also Margaret, who was Tom's age, Nancy, who was about a year younger than Mary, and Dorothy, younger still. It was a farm family, and like us, everybody had their farm chores.

John's dad had about eighty acres in various crops. It could have been more, and it seemed like the size of the world to this 12-year-old boy. There was always plowing, harrowing, cutting, or something that needed done. They had a John Deere tractor and the necessary implements to do those tasks. John was the primary driver and appreciated the relief.

I loved to drive that tractor. I liked going out there for that almost as much as anything else. When we got there after church on Sunday, we had a big breakfast then it was to the fields. John's Dad did the tough things, then turned the tractor over to us. As I said, I liked that, and at that age, I suppose if I could have just driven a tractor, I would have been a farmer the rest of my life. However, there are many other things a farmer has to do, most of which I didn't like.

Once I got on that tractor, it was awfully hard to get off and let John have a turn. I rationalized that John could go home every day after school and plow. I only got to do it on Sunday--once in a while. I had driven imaginary army tanks and flew imaginary airplanes winning the war, but this was real "hands on" experience. Those experiences taught me the basics of driving a car.

After about four hours of this, his dad would decide we had enough for a Sunday, and we would quit. Billy Buttress, another classmate, farmed across the road, and Jim Lea wasn't too far away. There were others in the area who were a year or two older or younger. We would all get together in the afternoon in someone's cow pasture, divide up sides, and play baseball or football.

Andy Griffith, in "What it was was Football," described the game, saying "They were trying to get the ball from one end of the field to the other without steppin in sumthin." That's the way it was. It was awfully tough to pick up a punt, or field a grounder right after it rolled through "sumthin." We played in jeans or overalls and T-shirts and run-of-the mill farm shoes. It is amusing to think that when a youngster suits up for a soccer game today, he puts on $50-$60 shoes, $50 uniform, warmup, rain jacket, and a bag to put it all in. He goes out onto a nice field, and doesn't have to worry about "steppin in sumthin." I know it is better now, but I think we probably had as much fun.

After the game, we cut a watermelon, or had something else, then it was time to go home. How fun those times were. We just didn't get to do it often enough, as far as I was concerned. As we grew older in school, John and I, with different interests, lost some of our closeness. John was active in FFA, and I was involved in band and football. However, I'll always treasure our relationship. At this writing, John and I are still friends, and communicate with each other about once a month.

Ruben Utley

When I was 12-13, Ruben was 25-30, I suppose. Ruben lived across the pasture in a house with his mother. Ruben was a "mental defective," as I remember him being called. In some movies, there is the "town idiot"---the guy who would do anything asked, but just wasn't wrapped real tight. That was Ruben.

He weighed about 200, was six feet plus tall, and strong as an ox. He could make good conversation, but his ability to reason was limited (that's my analysis). Some days, he could really impress you with his philosophy. I don't think we ever labeled him as a "crazy." It was that he was rather strange, and big.

He liked to play with us kids. We always enjoyed having him--at least until the point that he--not realizing his strength--would hurt someone. That seemed to happen frequently, ending the play period. We did everything outside--in the pasture, the yard, and in the barns. There was always a "catch me--you are it" type of game. Our pasture was dotted with wild plum trees. Those plums, when green, were great ammunition to use with our "nigger shooters" (described earlier). We used to have fights in the barns, around trees, etc. He was a big target, and rather slow, so we could hit him rather easily. However, Ruben was always a better shot, and usually ended up hurting somebody. That would end the game.

We played another game called "board behind." Somehow, we ended up with a bunch of wooden roofing shingles in our barn that were ideal for this game. One would take a board about 3-4 inches wide, about 2 feet long as his weapon. As long as he kept his backside covered with the board, he couldn't be hit. But the minute he uncovered to hit someone else, he was fair game.

We were playing this one day when Ruben came over and wanted to play with us. That was OK.

We were small enough, and fast enough to hold our own with him in that game. We kept out of his way, but those same abilities enabled us to sneak in for an opportunity shot. When two of us ganged up on Ruben, we always had the advantage. We could never hurt Ruben.

During one game I could hear Ruben's mother calling him. We told him but he paid no attention. After about an hour of playing, she appeared on the scene, really upset with him for not coming home. "But Mom," he said, "we were playing board behind, and I didn't hear you."

"I'll board behind you," was her response. With that, she picked up a 3-foot 1X4 and boarded his behind all the way home.

Ruben eventually got a motorcycle. He was so proud of it, and kept it polished so well. He didn't want anybody touching it. You can imagine what we did with that. He finally married a gal who was wrapped about as tightly as he. They left Broken Arrow, riding into the western sunset, but, eventually came back.

Ruben died at an early age, before I got out of high school. I think we were good to, and good for Ruben. We were never afraid of his mental problem--just his size. At times, we were cruel to him. For the most part, however, we cared for him, welcomed him to our activities, but often, we weren't so tolerant.

Counting Sheep

Counting sheep is a way for many to go to sleep at night. This has nothing to do with that except with regard to doing the counting, I went to sleep at the switch for a couple of days, and it was costly, especially to my brother Tom, and to me, to a measurement of my trust.

We raised sheep--not many, but perhaps 25-30. Tom had what many called a championship ram, which he was raising to show at the state fair that year. I had little to do with the sheep. They were Tom's. Tom arranged their breeding, was there in the night when a ewe was having trouble delivering, sheared them in the spring and sold the wool. Sometimes I could help tie the wool into bundles, and help dock the lambs' tails. I enjoyed watching the new lambs play.

My job, however, was counting the sheep at night to make sure they were all there and all right. I found, like other kids did then, and still do today, that I could cheat on responsibility every once in a while and get by with it. One time, however, it caught up with me. "Did you count the sheep tonight?" Tom would ask.

"Yeah, they are all there." I hadn't counted them. I got by with it. The next night, I thought I'd try it again. Just laziness.

"Did you count the sheep tonight?", again came the question.

"Yeah, they are all there." I hadn't counted the sheep.

The next night, Tom counted them. One was missing--his prize ram. We found it. We had an area below the dam of the pond where we dumped stuff that wouldn't burn. There was an old, rusted 55-gallon drum there with both ends out. Tom's ram had crawled into it--got hung up and couldn't get out, and in the heat of the next day, starved or died of thirst. I had failed in my job, then lied about it; and my parents and Tom lost some respect for me and trust in me. Tom lost his prize ram, and the ram had lost its life.

The sad part about it was that I didn't learn a lesson; or if I did, I forgot about it. A similar experience, if only relating to expected responsibility, occurred a year later, and we lost two piglets of a litter. It's an admittance that in each case, I failed--not failed, just didn't do it--then lied about it. I don't know why--my parents didn't raise me that way. That was hard to live with - - even harder years later as I write this.

We are told that we should take each bad experience in life and make something good out of it. I guess I eventually learned from this that no matter how minor a responsibility appears to be, someone is counting on it being carried out. If it doesn't get done, and that neglect is covered up, it will eventually catch up, and all persons involved will suffer.

The next year Tracy Hunsecker, a rancher down the road, hired me to count his cattle each night. He had some young calves, and there was always the fear of dogs or coyotes getting into the pasture and running the calves. Tracy had lost a calf earlier in the year. Dad was reluctant for me to take the job because of the past two experiences, but finally okayed it when I halfway convinced him that I had reformed. The job paid 15 cents a day I would be paid at the end of the month. I went to his pasture every evening before dark and counted the cows. When I was sure they were all there, I knocked on Tracy's door and told him. I did that for about a year.

Gene Flowers

Every town has a police force. The size of the town mandates its size. The wealth of the town mandates both the quantity and quality of police personnel and the vehicles they drive.

Gene Flowers was the Broken Arrow police force for as many years as I can remember. Gene was a huge, pot-bellied redneck cracker type of individual, with a big Luger, whose elevator did not always seem to go to the top. He was extremely bigoted, as many people were in those days, and he could be mean. I don't recall him liking many people, and I can't remember anybody liking him. You didn't want to cross him.

Gene drove his own car. It was probably the original version of the "plain brown wrapper car," a rust over brown mid to late 30's Hudson. He had no red flashing lights on his car. They would have been an unnecessary frill, as he couldn't catch anybody. A fast bicyclist would run him a good race. Everybody knew Gene's car. There was not another like it in town.

Gene kept law and order in Broken Arrow. He made sure the Negroes were out of town by sundown. He kept the kids in tow. He patrolled the streets at night, watching for speeders, peeling out, or cars with broken mufflers. He watched the two bars Saturday nights for drunks. It seemed his power and authority often went to his head. His office was a single room with a one cell jail in back. A rickety old sign hanging from the door marked the "Police Station," located in an alley, a half-block east of Main Street. It had no telephone. One wasn't really needed as there was no one to talk with.

When we delivered morning paper routes, we always folded them in the entry way of the post office on Main. That location would partially get us out of the winter north wind. Gene was always there to police us and make sure we cleaned up our mess. He would seldom talk to us, unless he had a complaint, but would just sit there in that old Hudson watching us.

In fairness, I guess I would have to say that Gene was successful. Broken Arrow was a peaceful town. On Saturday nights, I remember starting to deliver the Sunday paper shortly after midnight. The two bars on South Main were just closing. I remember seeing a lot of drunks, but rarely did I see a fight, or even hear a loud argument. He was awfully quick, without question, to escort a stranger to the edge of town, and tell him not to come back. Gene ruled, perhaps out of fear.

In spite of his good policing, there were two bootleggers operating in the Broken Arrow area. Since Oklahoma was "dry," the bootleggers did well. I believe they would even deliver. I drove through a drive-through once and asked for a fifth of something.

"Do you have an ID?" I was asked.

"I have five dollars," I replied.

"That's all the ID I need."

Gene didn't like Catholics. It was from him that I first heard the stories about "alcoholic priests" sleeping with the "whore nuns." It was almost as if there was a challenge when he told it. His attitude often did not make things pleasant for us. I remember hearing a story once that he threatened to shoot my brother Bill one time as a result of an argument. I know that one time in high school, my brother Tom picked up the nickname "Jailbird," and to this day, I have never learned why. I wouldn't be surprised if Gene Flowers had something to do with it. We Connerys certainly had a reckless reputation.

All-Night Parties

Occasionally, several of us boys had an all-night party. It was our version of the girls' slumber party. We would have had them more often if we could stay out of trouble and if our parents would have put up with it.

It was something to do in the summer--always at somebody's house with some degree of parental supervision and chaperoning. When at my house or at Jim Hocker's, who lived on an acreage farther out in the county, we slept in the barn. At other houses, we slept in the garage or backyard. We didn't want to be in the house, and parents, with some degree of reservation, were happy about that.

We played all sorts of games--had corn cob fights, blind man's bluff, etc. They always involved a lot of running and hiding, all after dark. Eventually, we would get settled in the barn, and talk the kind of talk young boys talk. We would go until sleep took over, and we always had a good time.

There were times, however, when there were problems. One time at my house, people in the new housing addition north of our property, called the police (Gene Flowers) complaining about window peepers. I don't remember who the two boys were, but we knew the people who complained, and the appropriate apology was made, and everybody was off the hook, even with Gene Flowers.

Another occasion, we were at Jim Hocker's. He lived two miles north of town on an acreage with a couple of out-buildings. It was another night in the barn with lots of room to run. I had to come into town at 4 a.m. to deliver papers, but intended to go back for breakfast after finishing my route, but decided to go home first. I was so tired when I walked onto the back porch, that I didn't realize the dutch-door into the kitchen was closed. It had a half window glass which I poked my head through. It just split the glass down the middle and woke me up. I realized I was through the glass and started to pull my head back. The two pieces of glass wedged on both sides of my nose, and the more I pulled, the more it cut, and the more it cut, the more I pulled. It almost shaved my nose to the bone. Several stitches and bandages later, I was all right. I didn't get back to the party. In fact, I spent most of the day in the hospital. It was about three days afterward that football practice started, and I was the only one on the team wearing a face guard. Now, everyone wears one.

On another occasion, we did the same thing at someone else's house. John Dale McCuistion (6'2" at 200 pounds) and I were at odds about something, and that was the night to fight.

"You wanna fight?" I shouted.

"Damn right," he responded. "I'm gonna whip your butt." And the fight was on.

In retrospect, it was really funny--we must have fought two hours with the rest of the guys egging us on. Mostly, it was a sparring match--we were both afraid of hitting one another--afraid that we might make each other mad. But, we fought. We both got some licks in, but never to the mouth or jaw. We didn't want to spoil each other's good looks. I think he probably won, but it was never really decided.

By this time, we were growing out of this stage, and we didn't have that kind of party again. I guess it was about the time we started getting interested in girls.

Bob Finkel Arrives

As I've said, we Catholics were a small minority in Broken Arrow. We were in real mission territory. We were ridiculed, often by people we thought were friends, and in many respects, they were. We were teased about how our priests were alcoholics, and slept with nuns. We were a little more than a step ahead of the Negroes, who had to be out of town by sundown. Much of this came down on us because of the Southern Baptist and Assembly of God beliefs, ignorance, and I believe in good part because of the attitude the church of always in praying for all those who were not Catholic.

In 1947 American Airlines moved their overhaul and maintenance facility to Tulsa from New York. Dr. Brissey, a dentist and dairy farmer and our neighbor to the north, sold a seven acre track adjacent to our property for residential development. Twenty-seven houses (I remember that number because I delivered papers to most of them) were built and many were bought by American Airlines people. Coming from New York, American brought us more Catholics, which bolstered our ranks, but there were no kids my age.

The move did bring us something else. It brought us Bob Finkel, a nice kid who was Mary's age. We liked Bob, as much as we did any of the other New Yorkers. But New Yorkers were just different.

Bob Finkel and his parents were Jewish. Maybe they were the first ones ever in Broken Arrow. It took the heat off us. I developed a lot of empathy for Bob. I knew what he was going through, because we had been through it. We, especially Mary, became good friends with Bob. But I think Dad and Mom had a problem with us associating with a

Jew. We never took part in any of the stuff that came down on Bob. We knew how much it could hurt. We had a lot of empathy for him. Still, we were glad the heat was off.

There was a time when Mary learned to drive and decided to take Bob for a joy ride. It was our 1948 Fleetline Chevy. I think Mary was 15 at the time and she might have taken the car without permission. It was one of those hot summer days when there was nothing else to do. Showing off, she tried to do a "whirly" in a gravel parking lot and turned the car over on its side. The car was back in the garage for repairs for a week or two. Fortunately, no one was hurt but it scared them badly. I don't think Bob ever rode with her again, but their friendship remained solid. Even though I was now the oldest one at home, I couldn't really criticize because I had banged up that same car a couple of times.

Ordering Groceries

Supermarkets had not found their way into small town Broken Arrow during the 1940s. And we didn't have convenience stores as they are known today. Three small grocery stores served the community and the surrounding countryside. Our shopping habits then were quite different than now. Except for canned goods, we ordered only a week's supply. We had no freezer and shelf space was limited. We shopped at Elmer Lloyd's grocery store and meat market. Elmer was a long-time family friend, and had a son and daughter in Tom's age group and a daughter in Mary's.

We had a standing rule in the family that when anyone was in town, he called before coming home to see if anything was needed. You might have to go by Lloyds' to pick up a loaf of bread, a can of beans, etc. The cost was always put on the tab, which was paid at the end of each month. There were enough of us doing this that it was rare to make a special trip to town for groceries. The napkins story contained elsewhere is one of those rare examples.

Mom rarely went to the grocery store since we didn't have a car, and working full time, she just did not have the time. Those rare times when she did go, one of us went with her and stuffed purchases into a bicycle basket to get them home. We bought weekly as our garden provided 90 percent of our vegetables that were either eaten fresh in the spring-to-fall season, or canned for the winter months. We always had our own milk and meat, which was eaten fresh, was cured, or canned. I often wish I had Mom's recipe for canned pork or beef. We had no freezer space, and I don't remember anyone else who did.

The Broken Arrow Ledger was published once a week on Thursday. Mom would compare her "needs" list with Lloyd's ad, and call in an order Saturday morning. There is a new trend now to do this same thing on line. Sometime Saturday afternoon, Elmer or one of his helpers would deliver. Groceries would be boxed or sacked and would be delivered in a pickup, often covered with road dust. Someone would sign the ticket, then there would be the routine of checking to see if we got all that we ordered. Rarely was there a mistake.

About 1947, the Farmers Market, the grocery on the south end of Main Street, opened a section for rental of frozen food lockers. They looked kind of like the morgue seen on TV programs today--the drawers were as wide and as high—but they were only about three feet long. We rented one, but continued buying our groceries at Lloyd's--customer loyalty, I guess.

That changed our whole way of eating. We could butcher beef or pork, have it cut and packaged, and put it in the locker. Mom and Dad began to do less canning, and we started freezing vegetables and fruit. This made things so much easier for them. Vegetables would be prepared, then taken to the Farmers Market for quick-freezing, then placed in the locker. We all had a key to the locker, and when calling home before leaving town, usually meant "picking up a loaf of bread at Lloyd's, and going by the freezer and get a package of ribs, a roast or whatever; and by the way, pick up a carton of frozen peas." It was really neat, after delivering papers in 100-degree summer heat, to go by the locker and cool off. It wasn't much fun in the winter. This was "uptown" living. Who would have thought, at that time, that one day, people would have a freezer in their home--much less a microwave oven. If Mom were still alive today, she wouldn't think of having a microwave, but that freezer was a blessing.

Mary and I with Andy
Circa 1945

The Family, Less
Mike and Bill

My Wheels, 1946

Bill Home On Leave, 1944

Mary on Pete, 1948

What's A Patio?

Two little six-year-old girls, Amy and Sally, were playing with their dolls. After they had put the dolls down for a nap, Amy said to Sally, "I found a condom on the patio this morning."

"I don't understand," Sally replied.

"I found a condom on the patio," Amy repeated with emphasis.

"I still don't understand. Wha . . .What . . .What's a . patio?" Times have surely changed.

There comes a time in a young man's life--I guess it occurs between 11 and 15. It's called puberty--it's called adolescence--it's called discovering, and appreciating, the difference between boys and girls-- and liking that difference.

I guess by today's standards and values, I had a tough time going through this period, although I didn't realize it at the time. It's called being dumb. There was a point in my life during those years, that I realized there was a difference, but I really didn't know what the difference meant. I didn't get a whole lot of help from my parents. If I could have talked to Dad about the scout camp incident, there might have been an opportunity for some learning. Sex was never discussed at home. I remember hearing, years later, a definition of sex, which was often told as a joke, but in the thinking of the times, especially Catholic thinking, carried a lot of truth: "Sex is an activity a husband and wife participate in, very quickly, in the dark, and only once per child." There wasn't even talk of, much less court cases, involving sex education in the schools. There was no TV where you could see it happening in prime time in the privacy of your living room. And, neither the movies nor the comics could show Blondie and Dagwood in the same bed.

So, there just wasn't much education about the birds and the bees as I went through that period. The above is not intended to be a philosophical discussion about the pros and cons of sex education of young adults--it's just to describe how it was. It would seem that in growing up on a farm, where cows, pigs and sheep were bred regularly, and a brood of puppies around most of the time, that there would be some understanding of sex. Not me.

One day during that period, I was talking to one of the "older boys," and he told me I needed to start carrying a rubber (now called condoms). He said, "You've got to get one John--you never know when you might need it."

I said "OK." I knew absolutely nothing about what a rubber was for, and wondered even more, how would I know when or where I would need it, or what I would do with it when the time came. But he was older, and wiser than I, so I figured it best to take his advice.

Nick Hood had a little corner store and gasoline station at the corner of 71st and Elm Place in Broken Arrow. It was a mile outside of downtown, and on the other three corners were farms. I knew Nick, because I delivered the newspaper to his house, and I had a news rack in his store. I was told he sold rubbers for a quarter. For some reason, I was embarrassed about buying one from Nick even though I had no idea what they were, what they looked like, or what they were for. I just knew that I needed to have one.

One day, when I took Nick's papers in, I bought one. When no one else was around, I whispered to Nick, "I need to buy a rubber." Nick had a sly grin on his face, and made some comments that I didn't understand, and sold me one. Nothing else was said. The next day, I couldn't wait to see the older boy, and show him I had taken his good advice. I tucked it away in my wallet, so I could get to it when the time came that I would need it.

After weeks of carrying it, and the normal wear and tear on my wallet, the familiar ring became obvious on the outside surface. It was much similar to the ring left on the hip pockets of jeans by those folks that carry Skoal, only smaller.

I was in--I was ready--whenever I needed it. In all honesty, my only reservation was the hope that some voice out of the sky would tell me when I needed it, and would also tell me what to do with it. I must have carried it two years--waiting. Then one day, some of our class were walking the distance between the junior high school and the auditorium at the elementary school, about 1/2 mile, and John Dale McCuistion got his out, filled it with water from a neighborhood garden hose, and threw it at a girl.

I thought, "Damn, is this what I've been carrying this for? Is now the time? Is that what they are for?" But I was restrained. I don't know why--whether I thought there would be bigger and better things, but I kept mine, safely tucked away in my wallet.

Not too long after that, my brother Tom--the same one who later confiscated the Saturday night beer and cigarettes (good old Tom was always looking after me), discovered the rubber in my wallet. "What are you doing with this?" he demanded.

I gave him that dumb "I don't know look," and said nothing.

I wanted to know what he was doing in my wallet. That's unimportant as there was no privacy at home. He gave me a stern lecture about the "wages of sin." I knew absolutely nothing about what he was talking about.

He gave the rubber to Dad, and Dad also lectured me--just before he whipped me good. He just wouldn't believe that I was just carrying it--waiting until the time I would need it--and that I had no idea under what circumstances I would need it. Another opportunity for a father-son talk was lost. I suppose that if it had not have been taken, I would have carried it another two or three years--waiting.

But with Tom's lecture, and Dad's lecture and whipping, I figured it must be bad, so I never replaced it. But the ring on my wallet was implanted, so, at least, I always looked like I was ready. There is another irony to this story. When I finally found out what it was for, and when it was used, I realized I could never use it anyway: I was Catholic. As time went by, the term "rubber" went out of style and became Trojan, a manufacturer's name.

Presbyterian Youth Group

Many of the social activities of this period centered around membership in church youth or other religious related groups. They were not too different than the church youth groups we know today. They were usually a Sunday School class which, along with guests, got together occasionally for various social activities such as skating or swimming parties, or other events.

There was also the Demolay, an organization for boys, which was sponsored by the Masonic organization; and the Rainbow Girls, sponsored by the Order of the Eastern Star, a women's auxiliary of the Masons. We Catholics could not belong to these organizations. As I understand it, it was not them who wouldn't let us in; but the Catholic Church, which prevented our participation. I always envied those kids because of that social contact.

As Catholics, we didn't have such groups. It was not that we didn't believe in it; it was that we just didn't have the numbers. In my age group, there was John Rodgers, who lived farther out in the country, Pat Moore, who we saw only on Sunday because he went to a Catholic school in Tulsa, my sister Mary, and Joan Monroe, a classmate of hers. In my early teen years, let's say 13-15, I got lonely for social contact. It was just a need to be with kids doing fun things outside of school.

Jim Hocker was a member of the Presbyterian youth group. He called about the middle of one week to ask if I would like to go on a skating party Friday night. I wanted to go, but I blew it off because I thought he was kidding--playing a joke, and because I just wasn't supposed to go. At 6 p.m. on Friday, he called to ask if I were going.

They were about ready to leave from the church, and I had not shown up. I knew he was serious now. I couldn't get there fast enough. I probably used the story I was going with the Hockers, which was not really wrong. I pedaled my bike as fast as I could downtown to the church. I got in the last car as it was pulling out. I guess there were about 20 boys and girls. I had never experienced anything like that and had a good time.

I came home, however, feeling a lot of recrimination. I had gone out with "them." I knew I was going to Hell; and what was more immediate, if Mom found out I had gone with a church group, I would have been in trouble right then. The fulfillment of a social relationship badly needed seemed to outweigh the forthcoming condemnation. So, I started making excuses on Sunday evening so I could get out and go to their youth group meetings.

They weren't so bad. There were always some religious teachings--some of which I accepted--some I didn't. But because of my religious upbringing, I always felt a sense of guilt about going, and before long, I stopped. I dutifully confessed my sins and felt better, but once again, I was, for the most part, socially alone.

The Ol' Swimmin' Hole

In the late spring and all through summer into early fall, we loved to swim. A lot of that seemed therapeutic because the summers were so hot. There was no air conditioned house to go into, and the only way to cool off, especially after a hard day's work, was to get wet. When younger, we got out the water hose, and splashed around. Even that proved dangerous at times.

We grew a little, and we wanted to dive and swim. The first stage of a 2-stage progression was Brissey's pond. We had a pond in our pasture, but it just wasn't fit to swim in, probably, because it was too shallow, and wasn't spring fed.

Dr. Brissey had a dairy farm to the north of us, and he had two sons, Max, who was Tom's age; and Gene, who was between Mary and me. Brissey's had a deep water pond north of their house, which was about a half mile from home. On a hot afternoon, cars and bicycles would be lined up along the road in front of the pond. These vehicles represented the kids' age span of 8-18 years. You had to climb through a barbed-wire fence, and walk about 150 yards to the pond.

We built a home-made diving board out of a 2X8, set it in place and swam. The big kids would sometimes pick on the little kids, but we all got wet, all got cooled off. Often, the cows would drink while we swam.

There was a problem associated with swimming - - and most other summer activities: sunburn. We Connerys were all extremely fair skinned and freckle-faced. One afternoon, bare skinned in the hot sun was all it would take. There was no way to work up to it - - 15 minutes the first day, 30 minutes the next and so on - - and end up with a great tan. Sooner or later, the burn would come, followed by the blisters. The cure for that, at least the treatment, was a vinegar rubdown at night. I remember nights when the whole house smelled of vinegar. But that helped subside the itching that followed the blisters. Then one would start the process again, to ease a summer-long problem.

The second stage was the coal pits. There had been a vein of coal about 2-3 miles east of us, which ran north and south for perhaps 10 miles. It had been strip-mined years earlier, and left a number of deep pits, some of which were at least a mile long. The water was deep, it was clear, and it was cold. There was a cliff to dive from, and we even put a jerry-rigged diving board out over the cliff, although it wasn't needed.

We spent a lot of afternoons there. On a hot afternoon, there was always time between the paper route and evening chores; and the choice was between Jack Hudson's or our house for a ball game, or the coal pits. The only problem was getting there. It was almost too far for a bike ride, but when we had to, we rode bikes over dusty gravel roads. Usually, we would find someone with a car and pile in--all ages, and go swimming.

We never had lifeguards there, or at Brissey's either. It was swim at your own risk. We did look out for one another, and it was always a basic rule that you didn't go swimming alone.

We had one coal pit that was our favorite. We called it "mile long pit," and it was close to being that long. Advanced boy scouts met their long range swimming requirements there. There was a high cliff for diving--and we soon learned that this was the easiest way to get in the water, as opposed to walking down the rocky path barefooted. I swam in that pit for three or four years, until it was time to go to college. The summer after my senior year was my last year of coal pit swimming.

My Show Calf

Tom got so much enjoyment working with, and raising livestock, that I decided that maybe I could find an interest in it. I had always been involved to varying degrees, but it was just a chore to me, and I did not enjoy it. There was no farming in my future. It was time, however, to give it a try. I would be 13 that year.

We had a beautiful Jersey heifer born early that spring. She was a beauty. O.L. Claxton, Tom's agricultural teacher, said she was one of the best looking heifer calves he had seen in years. She was mine.

We made plans early. I would raise her, and show her at the County Fair in the fall. I worked with that calf daily, and got excited about it. She had the right markings, the right physical build, the right mouth structure, the right carriage, and she grew and put on weight as she should have. As I worked with her, I could close my eyes and see myself leading a Grand Champion around the ring. I was proud of her. She would be about six months old at Fair time. That would put her in a specific bracket of the show.

Tom helped me a lot. He taught me how to stand her, lead her, and present her to the judges. He had done it before. The heifer and I both learned. Mr. Claxton even came by and gave his nod of approval. Everything went fine, until about a month before the Fair. She got sick. Two weeks later she was dead. Tom, Claxton, and the vet couldn't help her. Somehow, she got pneumonia in that hot August, and we couldn't stop it.

It was a disaster for me. After that, I completely lost interest in livestock again. It was relegated back to a chore.

Mutt And Keith

During the early part of my freshman year, I had two paper routes, morning and evening. Often, after finishing in the morning, I wouldn't get home before going to school, and when I did, it was usually just to pick up books.

Keith Boyce and Marvin (Mutt) White and I became good friends during this period, and their homes were near the end of my morning route. We would usually go to school together. Mutt played trumpet in the band, so my first contact with him involved music. Mutt's parents didn't like Keith. They thought Keith was not worth much, and that he was a bad influence on us. At one time, they forbid him to associate with Keith.

Mutt's parents operated the Farmers Co-op feed store in town, were very religious, and active in their church. I don't believe Keith's mother (his dad was long gone) had seen the inside of a church in a long time. Mutt was an only child, while Keith had twin sisters Velma and Thelma, two years older, and an older brother Mike's age.

Mutt was a straight arrow kid while Keith was always on the edge of trouble. They were both little--I was about 3 inches taller--and they weighed about 130 compared to 150 for me. However, Keith could be a bully to a 200 pounder. He was tough, and it was often difficult to keep that toughness in check. He didn't argue much--he went to the fighting stage rapidly. Keith was the kind of guy you were glad to have in your corner. They were both very bright and capable. Mutt applied it, and Keith didn't--too well, although I remember Keith winning the school spelling bee a year or two earlier.

Keith's mom was my second mom. She was a good-hearted, down to earth lady that had about the same education as my mom. She was a lot like my mom, and I guess that's why I liked her. She made the best pan biscuits from scratch that I have ever eaten--every morning. She always made us feel welcome. Mutt and I both called her our second mom.

Mutt was an early riser, and Keith was a late sleeper. I would finish my route, stop by Mutt's and we would go to Keith's together--or we would meet there. It took both of us to wake Keith up, and I'm sure that had it not been for us, there would have been many days Keith would not have gone to school. While we were pulling Keith out of bed---we always had to be careful, as it wouldn't take too much for Keith to come out fighting---Mom was making biscuits.

We would sit there every morning eating biscuits with butter and grape jelly as fast as she could make them in an open skillet. Occasionally there would be ham gravy to put on them. She was always pleased that we liked them so much. We went through that ritual almost every morning, then it was off to school.

When Mutt White, Keith Boyce, and I got together, life was never dull. We did the kind of things everyone else did, but for one reason or another, they always seemed to end differently. You could say we were trouble, or an accident, looking for a place to happen.

As we grew older, Keith, Mutt and I would pal around at night, especially on Saturdays. Keith, who worked at Stanfill's Grocery after school and weekends, had bought a hot '37 Ford coupe, that was robin's egg blue in color. We had transportation. It changed our lives. We began dating. Keith dated Shirley, a girl from Union High, a country school halfway between Tulsa and Broken Arrow. Mutt dated Barbara, a Tulsa girl. Barbara had fixed me up with her cousin. We had met them at the skating rink in Tulsa. It is amazing that all six of us could get into that car.

Whenever the three of us went out, Keith was "not with us," for Mutt's sake. I don't know what Mutt would tell his parents. We didn't ask. We managed to hide that for a long time.

Then one night: We triple dated that night--I don't remember what we did--went to a movie, or got a hamburger, or just went somewhere to park. There were lots of country roads to do that, How six of us could get into that car escapes memory, but we did. We had kissed the girls goodbye and were on our way home. My date lived the farthest so we said goodnight to her first, Then Mutt's, then Keith's. The only way to get back to B.A. was on country roads. We passed a parked car, which we thought belonged to Lee Neal, another B.A. student, and we honked, made some loud verbal comments and kept on going.

Pretty soon, that car was right behind us. We came to a stop sign and stopped. This guy rammed us. Into the back of Keith's Ford. "No one does that to me," Keith hollered. We all jumped out, ready to take on Lee Neal. Except it was not Lee Neal. I was the biggest of the three, being 6 feet tall and weighing about 150 pounds, soaking wet. Keith and Mutt were about the same size – three inches shorter and weighing about 130.

This guy came out of his car the biggest man I've ever seen--about 6'6", 250 pounds. As we used to say, he was big enough to go bear hunting with a switch. Moutain Man was what we called him later. He didn't have a switch, but instead, one of those 9-12 cell flashlights--about three feet long--in his hand.

There was never a word said. The first one into the fray was Mutt, and he caught the flashlight right across the mouth. Keith and I were right behind him, but we couldn't hurt the guy. I had a screwdriver in my hand, but could not hurt him with it.

Keith and I sparred with the guy for a few minutes (most likely seconds) when we noticed Mutt lying on the ground, his face covered with blood. The gal with the big guy had gotten out of the car to watch the slaughter, and I think she noticed Mutt first, and screamed. When Mountain Man saw Mutt, he couldn't leave fast enough. Keith and I were glad he did. We were in too much panic to get his license number.

We took Mutt to my house, got him cleaned up, and discovered a couple of teeth gone and two more hanging. I had to call his parents, and met them at the hospital. Somehow, we had to get Keith out of the scenario, and I don't remember how we did that.

Mutt played trumpet in the band, and played it well. We lost him for about four months while his mouth was being reconstructed and he was fitted for teeth.

There was a lesson there for all of us, but I'm not sure whether we learned it or not, and we continued to be friends and do the same type of thing that one way or another; sooner or later, got us in some degree of trouble.

Saturday Night In The Projection Room

For a town of less than 3,000 population, Broken Arrow was first class for entertainment. We had two movie theaters on opposite sides of Main Street in the same block. Both were owned by the Walker family. The NUSHO, a 1930s theater and the most modern of the two, was open seven nights a week and Saturday and Sunday afternoon. The "Old Show," appropriately labeled, had seen its better days many years before, and it was not uncommon to find a mouse between your feet eating popcorn. The Old Show was just open Saturday afternoons for grade B westerns.

Bob Walker, a classmate of mine, and his brother Bill, two years older, ran the NUSHO projection room on Saturday nights. Bob decided to make Saturday night a social event. Perhaps a half-dozen friends, all boys, would be invited to crowd into the small projection room to watch the movie. We always sat through it twice.

Invariably, about halfway through the first showing, we would pool our resources (usually all change) and would draw straws to see who went after refreshments for the second movie. We could always get popcorn, a soft drink and candy at the concession stand downstairs, but that wasn't what we wanted.

Our refreshments consisted of a six pack of beer and a pack of cigarettes. That was high living. Our source of supply was either Whitely's grocery store, about a mile south on Main where Highway 51 curved toward Coweta, or Nick Hood's on the other end of town. Either of these stores were "Mom and Pop" forerunners of the modern

7-11 convenience store, I'm sure ole man Whitely and Nick Hood saw through our "It's for Dad," or "My older brother is having a party" lines, but we would always manage to be convincing enough.

One night, I drew the short straw. Off to Whitely's I went on my bike. The basket on the front of the handle bars, which four hours later would be filled with Sunday newspapers, would hold the beer and cigarettes.

I used the "It's for Dad" line, while having a difficult time looking him in the eye, and I know he didn't believe me. But Mr. Whitely was a newspaper customer of mine--I had a rack in his store--so we knew one another well. He let me have it. Most likely I bought Falstaff beer and Chesterfield cigarettes.

Now, back to the NUSHO. I had to be careful with beer in the basket. I don't know if beer was in cans yet, but I had bottles. They rattled all the way. I didn't want to run into the police force--Chief Gene Flowers--or anyone else I knew, who might raise their eyebrows. Yet, for the first half mile, Main Street was the only way to go--and on Saturday night, the street was crowded. As I got closer, I could turn off onto a side street, but it would be two blocks farther on a gravel street and the bottles would rattle more.

I was doing fine until two blocks away from the theater, I ran into my brother Tom and two of his friends. Tom, four years older than me, was in college and home for the weekend. I tried to ride on past them but they stopped me.

"What's in the sack?" came the dreaded question.

"Oh, nothin," was my feeble reply as I tried to remain cool.

"Let's see." It was all over. I knew the "It's for Dad" line wouldn't work. Dad rolled his own Prince Albert, and rarely drank a beer he didn't make. Tom chastised me righteously on the evils of sin and the three confiscated my beer and cigarettes.

I'm sure the beer and cigarettes didn't go to waste--I'm also sure they were consumed that night.

I didn't have enough money to make another trip to Whitely's that week, and had an awfully tough time facing my friends. They gave me a bad time. It took me two weeks to pay them back, but I never had to make the beer run again.

The next morning, Tom told Dad the whole story; and Dad, after the lecture, whipped me. This was one of those times he would say, "I'm gonna slap you up to a peak, then slap the peak off." It would scare me to death, before the first lick. Drinking and smoking were definitely bad for my health. Tom had done it to me again. Sometimes, I wondered why I liked him so much.

The Gift Of Life

Mrs. Morse was an elementary school teacher, I think third grade. I never had her as a teacher -- and from the stories I recall, I considered myself fortunate. My only real contact with her during those early years was that I delivered her newspaper.

When I was about 14, her husband, Fred, got sick. I don't remember what his illness was, but it was a type of blood disease. It was such, that periodically, he would have to have his blood, at least partially, replaced for the rest of his life.

A call went out in school for blood donors. Even with the war, I had never heard of donating blood. Keith and I, along with two or three others, (can't remember who) said we would try it. I either lied about my age or forged a consent form--can't remember which. It was an opportunity to get out of school for a day and get a free steak dinner.

That first time was a traumatic experience. We were taken to Tulsa to donate, and were to have the steak dinner afterward. We were all apprehensive about what was ahead, and I'm sure each of us wished at times that we had not raised our hands. They had told us too many times that it wouldn't hurt--enough times to make us leery. But, we had gotten out of school, and the steak, seldom enjoyed, was ahead of us.

They were right. It didn't hurt at all. But, when coming down on the elevator from the fifth or sixth floor, the elevator stopped at the first, and I kept on going--out cold. When I got revived, I was ready for the steak.

Fred Morse and I found out later that we had the same type of blood--O-Negative, which is somewhat rare. Six people in 100 have it, also called the universal donor--it is compatible with any other blood.

That put me on the list. For the next four or five years, I got a call every three months or so that it was that time again. I would go to the local hospital and donate blood. I never had any hesitation about it after that first time, and it was always a tremendously good feeling to know I was helping keep him alive.

Fred and I became good friends. I would often stop and visit with him when delivering papers. Although Mrs. Morse was always grateful, we never had the friendship that Fred and I developed. That may have been me, not wanting to get too close to a teacher. I would often kid Fred that sooner or later, he would have to change his name to Connery.

It was during my freshman or sophomore year in college when I came home one weekend to find that Fred had died. How sad it was that he was taken. But the feeling was, and still is, that I had helped give him four years of life that he may not have had otherwise.

Sundays In Tulsa

The taste of big city life that I experienced in Tulsa during the summer visits to aunts and uncles made me want to go back. There just wasn't enough excitement in Broken Arrow, especially on Sunday afternoons.

I liked to roller skate, and I liked to watch the girls in bathing suits. So, on a lot of Sundays, Mutt White, Keith Boyce and I, and on other occasions someone else, would go skating, or swimming at Newblock or Crystal City amusement park.

Mutt would tell his parents that he had a ride with me--I would tell mine that I had a ride with him, and we would meet downtown and hitchhike. Today, there is an expressway that gets you to downtown Tulsa in 15-20 minutes. Then, it was country roads, and a state highway (not much more than a country road) which took 30-45 minutes to the outskirts. We would hitch along State Highway 51, passing Five Mile Corner, the County Farm, a small airport, Tulsa Memorial cemetery, then down 11th street to the skating rink. The skating rink used to be at the Tulsa fairgrounds, but had burned. If we were going to Newblock or Crystal City, on the west side of Tulsa, we would usually catch a bus or trolley once we got downtown.

One time, about age 15, I went by myself by that same method in the early morning to see my first niece, Diana, the first child of my brother Bill and his wife, Hildegarde. After visiting Hilda, still in the hospital, and seeing the babe through the nursery window, I went roller skating. There was a girl there whom I had met previously and we drank soft drinks and skated together. I got to walk her home. She lived only a few blocks from the skating rink. Her parents were not home and this gal knew more about the birds and bees than I did, and taught me a few lessons. I was so enthralled with her that I let the clock get away from me, and didn't start hitching home until about 6:30 p.m.

It took a while to get a ride, and it was about 8 p.m. when we passed by the school auditorium, and I wondered what all the cars were doing there. About midnight that night, I woke up, startled, remembering that it had been Baccalaureate services for the graduating class, Tom's class, and the concert band had played. I played timpani in the concert band and I wasn't there. I knew I was in trouble with Gesin.

I really had a tough time dealing with Gesin Monday morning. It was the only one of those Sunday trips that ended on a sour note, and it was the first band performance I missed. I never missed another.

We Make New Friends

It was about time to start school again. This would be a big year. First of all, I would be in high school--a freshman. Brother Tom was off to A&M to begin college and learn to be a professional farmer, and I would have my own room. Finally, there was the anticipation of making new friends and playing football.

Each freshman class got a new group of students. There were a number of dependent country schools around Broken Arrow that went only through the eighth grade. For the most part, these were one or two-room schools with several grades in one room. Those students came to Broken Arrow for high school. We were glad to get them because our class was rather small.

We added about 17 members to our class that year, from five different rural grade schools. The biggest was Lynn Lane, 6 miles to the north, where seven came from. There were Evans, Konklin, Oak Grove, and Weer independent schools, all 6 to 10 miles farther out in the county. Like most kids, most of the veterans and newbies were a little reserved about getting acquainted. Once everybody got past the shyness, we melded into a fine group, and developed some close friendships over the next four years.

These country kids (in this context I didn't live in the country because I didn't ride the bus) added a lot of class to our class. They represented themselves well. In our freshman year, Iva Mae Cates (Evans) was our valedictorian; Mary Blankenship (Lynn Lane) our football queen candidate; and Art Davis (Lynn Lane) and Lonnie Graham (Oak Grove) lettered in baseball. Art was president of our sophomore class, and he, Lonnie, and Glenn Cone (Konklin) lettered in football.

A bunch more lettered in various sports our junior year and Mary Blankenship was the FFA Queen. As seniors, Art Davis was vice-president and Lonnie was secretary-treasurer. We had our first student council that year and Art was elected president. Mary Blankenship was again recognized for her beauty and personality and was elected Cotton Queen and Sooner Princess candidate. Carl Clayton (Lynn Lane) was yearbook king. A year later, I would room with Carl at OU. Lonnie made All-State in football, and Glenn was selected All-Conference.

I probably have slighted somebody, and if so, that is regretted. I have only listed the above accomplishments to show what an impact these kids had on our school and class. These kids developed an attachment to Broken Arrow. They come back from places like California and Mississippi for class reunions, whereas many, who were in the school system many more years, and still live in Broken Arrow, don't come.

To The Showers

Football was my sport in high school. I never was very good, never got to play as much as I wanted, but I never stopped trying. I suppose I would have been better suited at playing basketball--I was tall, didn't carry a lot of weight, and was pretty fast--but I was also a little clumsy and didn't like basketball anyway. I had some good times playing football. It was an education in and of itself, and through it, I became much closer to some of my friends than I would have otherwise.

Football was big in Broken Arrow--as big as it could be in a town of 3,000. In the four years I played, we played in two difference conferences, and won the conference championship twice. But that is not what this is about.

It's about when I was a sophomore and out for football for the second year. I had been to a clinic the summer before, held by Head Coach Ragsdale and his assistants. That fall, I played tackle on the "B" team, today called junior varsity, and we had our own season of about six games.

We were playing our second or third game, at home, and our coach was Assistant Coach Joe Robinson, who was a classmate of Bill's, and later became the high school head coach then later, principal. It was a tough game, almost halftime, and the second team, which I was on, still hadn't gotten in the game. We were really needling Coach about letting us play.

At halftime, Coach Robinson really climbed on the first team for playing so poorly, then he climbed all over us for continuing to badger him about playing. He said if we didn't shut up about playing, he would send us to the showers.

Through the third quarter, the first team did a little better, and we were quiet. Then about two minutes into the fourth quarter, Art Davis got hurt. He was down on the field. I played behind Art. I got up off the bench, dropped my warmup, quickly loosened up, and told Coach I was ready to go. When he didn't respond, I said, "Coach, Art's hurt. Can I go in, huh, can I?"

He looked at me and shouted, "Yeah Connery, you can go in--to the showers."

It was the most embarrassing moment I ever had in football--walking up the sidelines toward the gate was a most humiliating experience, because in my mind, I knew that everyone knew. Actually no one knew, except Coach and a few others, trying to get into the game.

I came back the next day for practice. I had learned a lesson. So did the guys around me. Many would have quit. I thought about it, and I don't know why I didn't, except that I just wouldn't give up that easily.

Art was OK--not hurt too badly. We played together all through high school, with me behind him most of the time. He went on to play at Tulsa University, and was voted outstanding freshman athlete. He was severely injured in his sophomore year, and dropped out of football except for kicking extra points and field goals. He career was in coaching high school football after graduating from college.

I was kidded about the showers incident for what seemed like months. That didn't help my attitude, but, before long, it was someone else's turn to screw up, and I was off the hook.

What Ever Happened To Pep Clubs?

In later years, I enjoyed going to my son's and nephew's football games. I enjoyed the long runs, good passing, the fourth and ones, and the good defenses. I enjoyed the bands, the cheerleaders and the hot dogs. But something was missing. Where was the pep club?

When football season started, it seemed that everyone in high school was involved. It was said that if you didn't play football, you played in the band. But there was more to it than that. The FFA (Future Farmers of America) combined with the homemaker's class to run the concession stands at the games, helped by parents and sponsor teachers. Other school groups did other things. But what about the girls: pep clubs. We always had a pep club when I was in school. That's who the cheerleaders led in cheers. It was a school activity and they practiced most every day, just like the band and football team.

Everybody in high school belonged to something--band, football team, flag corps, cheerleaders, and pep club. Almost everybody had a part to play at a football game, and the week before to practice. Football was an all hands operation.

The pep club had about 40 girls. Boys did not become cheerleaders in Broken Arrow. The girls wore a uniform of sorts--black skirt, gold sweat shirt (school colors) and saddle oxfords. They had a faculty sponsor, and were led by the cheerleaders. Cheerleaders were selected from pep club ranks. The pep club had a place in the end zone bleachers, next to the band.

They took a lot of pride in their organization, and most often made enough noise to get the rest of the crowd going to help the football team get up when they were down. They had their own bus (a regular school bus) to travel to games, and always went as a unit, caravanning with the band bus, and often the team bus. We (band, pep club, and sometimes the team) always stopped to eat after an away game. It was always fun, especially when we won. For the guys (and gals too), if in the band or pep club, it was always an effort to swing getting your girlfriend on the same bus coming home. Most found a way, which made the trips a lot more fun. Coach prohibited football players from dating. If caught with a girl you could expect to run extra laps for the next week or so.

Where there is a will, there is a way. Football players who had a car would park by the band room when they came to prepare for a game. On away games, the pep club and band would usually get back before the team. Girlfriends would hide in the back seat of their guy's car until the player had safely driven away from the school.

Times surely have changed. In our day, boyfriends, for the most part, were either on the team, in the band, or selling hot dogs at the home economics or FFA stand. There are just so many things like this that were such a big part of life then, which have now disappeared. Perhaps I'm just an old man talking, but young kids just don't know the good things they are missing.

Buck

Herman K. Ragsdale was head football coach at Broken Arrow during my junior high and high school years. He was a good coach. During those years he had his share of conference championship teams, two of which I played on. During my first two years in high school, he was also principal.

Herman was also a whittler. At football games, the team manager was responsible for placing a bag of pine 2x2's, about a foot long, under our bench with the ball bag. At kick off, Coach would take out his Case pocket-knife, with a 3-4-inch blade, a 2x2 and whittle throughout the game. The closeness of the game could be determined by the amount of wood chips along the bench. The home bleachers were right behind the bench, and usually packed with fans. If things were going bad, and a fan behind the bench would start yelling at Coach, he would turn toward the fan, knife in one hand and board in the other. The look in his eyes told the fan not to yell again.

However, this is not about football. This is about Herman K. Ragsdale. Herman was a few years older than brother Mike, class of '31. He also was a Broken Arrow product, and as I understand, was quite a good football player. As Paul Harvey would say, this is the "rest of the story."

When Herman was tearing up and down the football field, he was also doing many of the things we did when we were kids, and often times, ending up in trouble. Like the time Tom and I went out to steal a water melon, so did Herman in his day. On one occasion,

Herman wasn't so fortunate. He got caught, so the story goes. The farmer allegedly peppered him in the butt with a shotgun.

I've heard that it didn't hurt him that badly--more his pride than anything else. Old timers (before my time) like to tell the stories about Herman being laid out on a pool table at the American Legion Hut, buckshot plucked from his backside while onlookers drank warm beer.

From that time on, Herman earned, and well-deserved, the nickname "Buck." As it came down through the years, however, only his peers and elders used that word. God help any student who did. A student would need all the help he could get. Then I came along.

Coach Ragsdale (we were allowed to call him by his first name--COACH) conducted a football clinic in the summer. It was his way of preparing kids for the 2-a-day practices in the heat a week or so before school started. I was going into the ninth grade, a freshman so I was out for football. The older boys told me I could call him Buck. Why, did I always listen to the older boys? I did.

He was friendly, gracious, kind, and seemed accepting, with a big smile. He didn't say anything about the name. I don't know why, except perhaps the clinic was not school sponsored. I thought it must have been OK. However, when school started that Fall, he came down on me like a ton of bricks.

I'll never forget that day. There was a circular drive that went around the 3-story high school building. Immediately in front of the building, on that drive, were a half dozen parking places where the school VIPs parked. Herman had a parking place there. Between those parking places and the school was a long, wide sidewalk to the front door. At the parking area end of the sidewalk were four or five posts--across the sidewalk entrance for pedestrian traffic. It was almost like four turnstiles, without the turnstile gates.

I was coming back to school on my bike, after having been home for lunch. I had cut across the school grounds and was approaching that entrance just as Herman, Joe Robinson, his assistant, and Red Rogers, another coach, were getting out of the car, returning from lunch.

I was about to pass between two of the posts when I waved, and said, "Hi, Buck." That's all there was. He grabbed me by the shirt collar with one hand, the belt with the other, and jerked me off the bike, leaving it banging between the two posts. He dragged me 50 feet down the sidewalk, into the building, up the stairs to his office, and paddled me good with a 3-inch-wide board. Fortunately, he didn't use the one with holes in it, as he was rumored to have. He warned me to the point just short of death, what he would do if he ever even heard of me saying that word again.

It was humiliating to walk down that sidewalk and pick up my bike, still lying between two of the posts. My pride was shattered. He got my attention. Two days later, I was back in his office again. He chewed me a new one, because a friend of a friend of his heard from someone that I was using that name behind his back. That was not true, but the incident further got my attention. For the next four years, I toed the line. In my junior year, he stepped down as principal, but remained the football coach.

If you worked hard in practice, you got to play. To Letter, one had to play in 16 quarters. I don't know how Coach kept track of it but he did. I barely made it my junior year, playing second string, and putting on that jacket was one of the proudest moments of my high school years. He was still Coach.

Many years later, in 1969, when I came back to Oklahoma for my mother's funeral, I visited Fred Gesin, who had been our band director. More about him later. As we visited on his front porch, where I once threw the Tulsa Tribune, Gesin was waiting on a ride to an educational seminar. The ride turned out to be Herman Ragsdale. As we stood in his front yard, I in uniform, a Navy Lieutenant Commander, when Herman drove in and got out of the car. I walked up to him, shook his hand, grinned, and said "Hi, Buck." He grinned as we shook hands.

I had reached peer status.

Years later my brother Tom invited me to a luncheon-reunion at his home for his high school class. Here were the football players I admired growing up. Fullback Les Randall, end Tom Dark, running back Johnny Montgomery and others. Also in attendance was Coach Ragsdall, now totally blind. The admiration and respect they showed this man was amazing. When they spoke, he knew who they were. And each of them, when they could get him alone, was like a young boy going to confession: "Coach, I'm so sorry I dropped that pass in the last quarter of the Claremore game."

"Coach, forgive me for fumbling the ball on the goal line against Sand Springs. No mention of "Buck." No mention of "Herman." Just "Coach."

Hunting

All of us boys, at one time or another, hunted. I never got too serious about it, and pretty much limited my activity to rabbits, ducks and, occasionally, geese. Tom, on the other hand, liked to hunt quail. My hunting days ended when I started college.

Dad taught me the basic "how to's" and safety of using a shotgun at about the age of 12. He had a single shot, 28-gauge shotgun that was my favorite and was ideal for rabbits. It was a rare gun--they hadn't been made in years--and it was difficult to find shells. I remember, we had been out hunting one time, and when returning, stopped by a little country store. The owner had about 20 boxes on the shelf that he couldn't get rid of and we bought all of them. Those lasted us a few years.

Rabbit hunting was my favorite because it was so easy. Out the back door into the pasture, and adjoining pastures and I was in rabbit territory. It was so convenient to go out for an hour, two hours, or I could make it an all-day trip.

Dad went with me a few times, and I went some with Tom. When they were satisfied that I knew how to respect and handle a gun, I was able to go by myself. I did that quite often, especially after Tom started to college. Dad had taught me how to carry a gun; how to, on quick notice, bring it to firing position; and how to lead a rabbit or a bird. He never liked us to shoot at a sitting animal. "Give it a chance," he would insist. He always taught me to unload the gun before climbing over a fence. When we came home, and passed through the gate into the back yard, the gun was unloaded.

Dad also had 12-and 16-gauge shotguns, which were a little bigger than the 28, and they were pumps. We used these to hunt ducks and geese. Tom had a friend who lived along the Arkansas River outside of Jenks. He had a duck blind on the river, and in the fall, usually around Thanksgiving, we would go there.

Bobby Reeves, one of the American Airlines people living in the housing addition next to us, became a good friend of the family. He was always grateful to Dad, as Dad had taught him many things about Oklahoma living that he didn't need to know in New York. Bobby and I would go up to Brissey's pond in the fall looking for duck. I remember one time we positioned ourselves on opposite sides of the pond below the bank, knowing there were some ducks on the water. When the ducks took off, we came up firing, just as they were clearing the water. We were shooting directly at one another. We didn't get a duck, but we peppered each other with buckshot. We were so far apart that neither of us were hurt, but we did learn a lesson. Another favorite hunting partner was Keith Boyce. We liked to rabbit hunt together, but a lot of times, we would end up shooting at tin cans.

Quail hunting was always a favorite around the house in September, although I never cared much for it. Uncle Horace Wilson, Dad's brother-in-law, had an excellent birddog, Andy, and kept him at our house year round so we always had a hunting dog at our disposal, but rarely used him. Uncle Joe Eustice, Mom's brother, would bring his bird dog out for a day and we would all take to the woods. Horace and Joe were both excellent hunters. Dad liked to quail hunt also, and before he got sick, was probably a better shot than they were.

One year, when Andy was getting older, about the time Tom was a junior in high school, Andy took to wallowing in cow manure. He looked for the fresh stuff. He would roll in it and come to the house, wanting dinner and wanting to be petted. He was always a mess and would smell up the whole back yard. We would hose him off and he would go do it again. Finally, Tom figured out a solution. We took two long ropes and fastened each to his collar. Tom would take one rope and I the other, and we would walk around the pond, dragging Andy through the pond. Back and forth a couple of times and that would clean him up. After doing that a couple of days, Andy stopped wallowing in cow manure.

We did a little bit of fishing, but were never serious about it. Our idea of fishing was a cane pole, a can of worms, and a pond or creek. As I got a little older, a girlfriend and a six pack were added; and it didn't matter whether we caught fish or not.

My favorite was frog hunting. All the farm ponds around were loaded with bull frogs. It was fun to go out at night and gig frogs. Not much was required--a bright flashlight, gunny sack, and a gig, we would make from an old broomstick and nail. Occasionally, we would use a small boat, but most of the time, we would hunt from the bank. When you got that light in the frog's eyes, it seemed like he would go into a trance and just sit there. That made it easy to gig him and get him in the sack. Frog legs the next morning were excellent. I taught the husbands of two elementary teachers to frog hunt and they went with me regularly.

Booster Trips

Broken Arrow had two big celebrations each year. Rooster Day was in the spring and Cotton Jubilee was in the fall. Like any other agricultural community, we celebrated the end of the growing season, the harvesting of the crop, and the success and sometimes failure of that harvest.

These celebrations originally had a two-fold purpose--(1) to bring people, who had struggled individually during that season to keep their heads above water, together for a social celebration, and (2) to promote the town, and bring business into town. All Oklahoma towns had their own unique 3- or4-day celebrations. A traveling carnival would come to town, there would be a parade featuring neighboring bands and floats, and fiddling contests. A western swing band like Johnny Lee Wills, or Leon McAuliffe would do their Saturday radio broadcasts from the Main street stage and climax the event with a Saturday night street dance.

Broken Arrow always conducted a booster trip for each of these celebrations. Booster trips were sponsored by the Chamber of Commerce. A caravan of cars left early Thursday morning, and visited all the surrounding communities to promote all the hoopla of the forthcoming weekend celebration.

A sort of select band had a part in this trip each celebration, and it was something to look forward to. I say "select" because we traveled light. It was kind of like a jazz band, except bigger. Perhaps 20 pieces. It was always a "hard day's night," to paraphrase a Beatles song title.

Between Chamber of Commerce speakers who drummed up the

event, the band would play. It was always fast paced. We would never spend more than 20-30 minutes in one town. Here and gone. I suppose that through previous arrangements with town officials, there was a time schedule which we had to keep. We made enough noise coming into any town that I believe locals would have wanted to know when we were coming. Most of the time was spent driving from town to town.

We would always hit a Tulsa radio station at noon and have a 15 minute live spot from a street curb. That's when a drum head would break--a clarinet reed would split, or one of the trumpet players couldn't find his mouthpiece. We never worried about sheet music--we didn't need it so we never took it with us. We would play about four or five tunes in each town-- about eight towns, plus the Tulsa radio program.

There were usually about 20-30 cars in the caravan. Each would be decorated with colorful crepe paper, much of which would be gone by arrival in the first town. Band members would find a car at the beginning and stay with it all day. Invariably, there was always a fender bender, a flat, or an engine that stopped running; and we would regroup as necessary. At some point, it seems, it would always rain and we would get wet, instruments and all. But the show had to go on, and it did.

There was a "chuckwagon," a trailer pulled by a car, or a pickup, and somewhere on the run, we could grab a bologna and cheese sandwich, drink and chips. It was always rumored that the men (seldom did a woman go) had a cache of beer in someone's car, and perhaps something stronger.

I made those trips for three years, and each successive trip, I learned to have more fun. We "old timers" in the band could really ham it up. Most of the trips, in my memory, have merged or faded into one trip. But there is one I'll always remember.

I rode with Harry Kates, publisher of the Broken Arrow Ledger. His son, Jerry, played trombone. It rained all day. After the last town, we were on our way home in a driving rainstorm, and Harry had a blowout. I think I was the only one who knew how to change a tire; or at least, that's what they led me to believe. I had the car jacked up, and was putting on the spare when the car carrying Fred Gesin, band director, drove by. They stopped, he opened his window, saw what I was doing, and said, "Band practice at 8 p.m. Don't be late."

I wasn't late. This trip had been on a Thursday, and the next day, the concert band was going to Tahlequah, some 45 miles away, for Regional Band contests. So, Gesin had scheduled a final practice that night. We had been wet and cold most of the day. Drum heads were broken and needed to be fixed. Trumpet lips were split, needed a rest, and could not be repaired so easily. Everybody was exhausted.

We didn't get much practice in that night. Gesin told us we were good enough to do it. We believed him.

The bunch of us, all dried out and looking smart in our uniforms, melded in with the rest of the band and got first place, both in the concert and marching contests.

Things have changed over the years. There is no more Cotton Jubilee. I don't think cotton is even grown in this part of the country anymore. Rooster Day is still held every spring, but the Booster Trips are gone forever, and have been replaced by class reunions over the weekend.

The Day Dad Died

Not long before Christmas, 1949, Dad got sick again and returned to the hospital. He had heart problems, and was having difficulty breathing. He always seemed congested, which was a fallout from the tuberculosis, and having only 1/4th of normal lung capacity. He was 56 years old. He went into the Veteran's Hospital at Muskogee, about 60 miles from home.

Over the next few weeks, Mom stayed there off and on, and occasionally, Mary and I would get to go visit him. We spent Christmas Day at the hospital, and it was easy to see that Dad was fading. In January 1950, he got worse. On about the 28th, Mom was called and told that he didn't have much longer. She and the rest of the family left for Muskogee. Tom came from school at Stillwater. Mike and Bill were both here. I was left at home as we still had some animals to care for, and I had to deliver newspapers every day.

On the 30th, at about noon, I decided that I would cut school early, get my paper route delivered, feed the animals and hitchhike to Muskogee. If everything went OK, I could be there by dark. I wanted to see Dad one more time. As the afternoon progressed, going became more important to me. I cut school about 1:30 and delivered my route in record time. I would be home about 3:30, and could be on my way by 4:30. I was kind of excited about making such a trip--a little apprehensive about it, too--because I had never hitchhiked that far.

When I rode in the driveway, there were about five cars there. Everyone had come back. I wondered why? As I got closer to the house, it dawned on me. I knew. Dad was dead. I didn't want to go in the house. I didn't want to hear those words. I didn't want to face it. I finally got the courage to walk through the door. Mom had told everybody that only she would tell me. I spoke to Tom and Mike, and I think Aunt Rose, and no one said anything. I didn't hear those words. Maybe he had gotten better. Then, I saw Mom. She put her arms around me and said, "Daddy's gone."

I was 15 years old with no father. In fact, for many years, because of Dad's condition, I hadn't had the kind of father my friends had. This is not a put-down to my Dad, but that was the way it was. It was just too bad that Dad and I had never had any of the growing-up conversations that are important to a young boy's development. Tom pretty much took over as the male role in my life. Despite what had happened in the past, I looked up to him. Tom officially assumed the role that day. He took charge of me. He held me, comforted me, and said things would be all right. He took me to town, just to get away from the house. I think he wanted a beer, but I was too young.

We parked on Main, and the first person I saw was Joan Holiday, a classmate and friend of mine. She was walking down Main. I went up to her, put my arms around her, and said, "My Dad is dead." It was verbalizing the fact to someone else that brought it home to me. I believe, at that time, I accepted it.

The next three days were miserable. There were still chores to do, newspapers to deliver, friends and relatives to see, to cry with. Time to look at my brothers or my sister without crying. Time to hold up Mom and be held by her. At the same time, I had to feel some relief. He would no longer "slap me up to a peak then slap the peak off."

We had Dad's funeral in St. Anne's Catholic Church, and buried him in the family plot at Calvary Catholic Cemetery in Jenks. I learned later that a large number of my classmates attended the funeral. I guess I was in so much of a daze that day that I didn't recognize anyone. I just remember the little church being packed. For most of them, it was their first time in a Catholic church, and most had talked to our English teacher, Willie Kennedy, about what to wear, what to expect. Even 37 years later at a class reunion, I appreciated hearing that. As was the custom, the funeral procession went through downtown Broken Arrow on Main Street, then on to Jenks. One pass through the streets to let people say their goodbyes. I remember the men on the street stopping and taking their hats off as we went by. Traffic seems so heavy any more that this doesn't happen.

After Dad was gone awhile, Mary, now 13, moved into his room. Now, Mary and Mom had their own rooms. On a cold night, I still had to go through Mom's and Mary's room to get to the bathroom. I could go through the kitchen and back porch.

It was tough going back to school. We were starting a new semester. A month earlier and we would have been in the midst of finals. Not many months after that, Art Davis, a classmate and close friend of mine, lost his father, resulting from a sudden heart attack. What I had been through enabled me to be a help to Art.

Off To War Again

Mike and Bill had been home from World War II three or four years. Both were attending Tulsa University, working on degrees. Later, Mike attended Purdue University and Oklahoma A&M, working on his masters degree.

Bill got married in 1948, and his wife, Hilda, became pregnant. Mike got his masters degree in January 1949, and got married that month. He went to work to start a new life. We were all excited about the new in-laws, the new niece, and the fact that Mike and Bill were on their way in life.

Then in June 1950, the North Koreans crossed the Yalu River into South Korea, and the United States entered into a Police Action. My old WWII favorite, General MacArthur, was there, and soon, we saw Mike's and Bill's name in the Tulsa Tribune as being recalled to active duty. There was a long list of names each day, and most saw it in the newspaper before they were officially notified. When they came home after the war, they still had a reserve obligation to fulfill, and the reservists were the first to go. Bill was able to get out after a couple of years, but Mike decided that the Navy would be a good career, got a commission in the Medical Service Corps, and stayed 30 plus years, retiring as a Captain.

The two blue stars went back into the window again, and as before, we said prayers that we wouldn't have to change them to gold.

As I got a year or two older, many of my friends joined National Guard Units, and some of those units were activated. Those guys, however, had the option to go or not go because they were still in high school. Val Jean Dorrell, in the class ahead of me and brother to my classmate Fred, went on active duty and was killed in Korea. Tom graduated in 1952 from Oklahoma A&M, was commissioned in the Naval Reserve, and he went. I don't know if we added another star or not--Bill may have already been out.

When I entered the Navy in 1956, the Korean War was all over. But I had two deployments to the Tonkin Gulf in the Vietnam War, got to see the Suez Crisis, Bay of Pigs, and Cuban Missile Crisis.

What does all this mean? Why have we, for years, gone off to foreign shores to fight what many people call someone else's war or interfering with another country's internal problems? The reason is that we are free. Freedom is not free. And we must, on a long range basis, go where we have to go, do what we have to do, to protect that freedom, and foster the idea of freedom elsewhere.

We hear a lot today and in previous years about the stigma of the Vietnam Veteran. (I am one of them). As we used to say in the Navy, "We were screwed, blued and tatooed," both while over there and after we came home. When I came back from my last Vietnam deployment, I settled in Silver Spring, Md. for duty in Washington. For the first three to four months, when my children went out to play, all of the neighborhood children were called in because I was a "trained killer." It was a political decision to enter that war. History books won't call it a war, because it was never "declared." But the effects on the people involved were the same.

We came home, not as heroes, not as defenders of our country, but as trained killers who had gone out and used that training. I don't argue the political decision to enter the Vietnam War. What I do argue, is that after that decision was made, they would not let the military fight the war, using military logic. Civilians who weren't there, who knew little about any existing situation, who knew nothing about the strategy of battle, sat back in Washington, pulled the strings and called the shots. I saw too much of that when I was there.

But enough about war. To discuss the pros and cons about war is not the purpose of this book. However when I consider that during the 18-year period of this book (1934-1952), we had been at war six years, one third of the time, it becomes a big factor in the lives of a country. And it was much because of that that this would become my occupation, my profession, and my vocation for 21 years. The best thing that I can say is that these wars have been someplace else, not in our own country.

Draggin' Main

The big night in Broken Arrow, like in other small towns, was Saturday night. We had the American Legion Hut, another bar, two cafes, two movies, two drug stores, and a Dairy Queen. Occasionally, a big tent came to town and set up on North Main Street, housing either a skating rink or a revival. It seemed like it was always the same tent. What I've described here is Broken Arrow in my later teen years. In times previous, we didn't have the cafes, the drug store was closed and we didn't have the Dairy Queen.

Saturday was a time, however, when everybody came to town--from all over the country side. Many brought their commodities such as eggs, vegetables, etc to sell in booths; others to shop, and many just to look at the bright lights and visit--the "spit and whittlers."

By 4 p.m. on Saturday, you couldn't find a parking place in the 4-block stretch of downtown main street. People would park early to be assured of a parking place, then do the things they came to do. In earlier times, parallel parking was allowed in the center of Main street, but those spots had been eliminated. The early evening was time for socialization, and they would either walk the street and visit with people, or sit on their fenders awaiting people to come by to visit them.

While all this was going on, there was a traffic jam in the street. Cars were filled with high school kids like me, and it was called "draggin' main."

Most parents had said, "Yes, you can go out, but DON'T leave town. So, there we were--somewhere between the Assembly of God Church at Main and Detroit on the North end, and Main and Freeport at the railroad crossing to the South, at best a half mile. Along that route, we passed all the things previously mentioned, two banks, furniture store, lumber yard, two clothing stores, Dr. Polk's office, the post office, two barber shops, a couple of car dealerships, and sundry other businesses.

Go to one end, make a U-turn, and go to the other. Back and forth, each time waving to a friend going the opposite direction, and occasionally, someone along the sidewalk. Back in those days, cars would get about 25 miles to the gallon, gas was 17 1/2 cents a gallon, and the movie cost a quarter. So, it always seemed an economical form of entertainment. It was a way of life.

I think it was right there in Broken Arrow where the "Where did you go?"

"Nowhere."

"What did you do?"

"Nothing," routine originated.

Every once in a while, someone would forget (or ignore) the "Don't leave town" rule and a car load or two would go to T-Town, or perhaps Bixby or Jenks. In Tulsa, there were drive-ins where we would get a hamburger, fries and coke and watch the girls. In Jenks and Bixby, there were only girls to watch, and not many of them. In these two cases, the Arkansas River was the dividing line, and often, we'd get run back across the river by some of their guys. We did the same thing to them when they came into Broken Arrow for the same reasons.

One Saturday night it happened to me. I had the car. We were draggin' Main. It was about 11 p.m. and I had about two hours to kill before the Sunday newspapers arrived. Not really enough time to go home and sleep.

Someone said, "Let's go to Boman's and get a hamburger." Boman's was a drive-in at 31st and Sheridan in Tulsa. At that time, it was a long way out in the country from downtown Tulsa. The only thing between Broken Arrow and Boman's were country roads. It was a place we often went when we had transportation. There were four of us--Joe Aud, a class ahead, Keith Boyce, Royce Grubb, a class behind, and me. Keith and I had been good friends for a long time. The other two were friends, but we ran with different crowds. I don't know what brought the four of us together that night. Most likely, it was the car.

We went to Boman's and had our hamburger, fries and drink. We flirted with the car hops and girls in other cars; and visited with some friends we saw. It had been a fun but uneventful evening. It was time go--I had work to do back in Broken Arrow. We were on our way home, but we drove a different road, a country road I hadn't driven before. I remember this trip so clearly.

We had just heard a public service message on the car radio, reminding drivers to dim lights when there was approaching traffic. I had heard this message two or three times and automatically dimmed my lights when I saw the car coming. He didn't dim. As I got closer to the car, I flashed my lights a couple of times with no response; and I noticed that he was in the center of the road and driving very slowly. I had to get off the road to avoid him, and Joe Aud, sitting in the front seat, hollered, "Look out for the bridge!"

The car had stopped in the middle of the road, on the middle of a creek bridge with his brights on. I had two choices--him or the bridge guard rail. I took the latter and really creamed the right front fender. When the dust settled, Joe, who had hit the windshield and was still in somewhat of a daze, got out of the car on the right, and immediately dropped about 12 feet into the creek bed. He was the only one hurt.

We didn't know how badly--he was extremely dazed and disoriented from the two sudden stops. I guess I was too because I did not insist on exchanging information, as was taught in Driver's Ed. The guy in the other car agreed to take Joe to the hospital, and Royce went with him. Keith and I stayed to await the highway patrol and get pulled off the guardrail.

We described the accident to the Highway Patrol Trooper, and he asked if we had gotten the other guy's name or license number. We had not. He wrote an accident report, and we got pulled off the guard rail. The car was drivable, and we didn't know about Joe or Royce, or even which hospital they were going to. There wasn't much point in waiting there, so I drove Keith home, delivered my papers and went home.

I didn't want to tell Mom about wrecking the car, but obviously,

I had to. It was a tough thing to do, and I know she was angry, and disappointed with me. I wasn't supposed to leave town that night. The four of us got together Sunday morning, and we found out that Joe was all right. When finished at the hospital, Joe had called his sister and she had picked them up. At the worst, it was a mild concussion.

I don't say much about my brother Bill in this book. To do so adequately would double the size of this volume. Suffice it to say that Bill did a lot of good things--and a lot of things not so good. This is about one of the good things that directly involved my life. I had told him about the accident, and he wanted to be part of the meeting. The trooper had indicated in the report that, if what we said was true, the other driver bore some responsibility for the accident. Bill wanted to find out who he was.

In our meeting, we discovered that the other guy had dropped Joe and Royce off at the Emergency Room door of St. John's hospital, and left. He didn't even get out of the car. They had to call family to come get them and pay the bill. Before going to the hospital, however, the driver had taken his lady friend home in South Tulsa. Royce thought he could remember where the house was and find it.

Bill, Joe and Royce were off. After some searching, they found the house, talked to the lady, and found that the guy who had been out with this lady was married to someone else. Bill put the screws to them--hard enough to get everything paid for, including Joe's medical expenses. I guess one could call it blackmail, and perhaps it was. Bill could do that sort of thing well.

Needless to say, but this ended, for what seemed to be a long time, my draggin' Main.

The World Of Work

There was always work in my life. It was part of life, like eating or sleeping. Mike, my oldest brother, was 12 when Dad got sick. He and Bill, 11, were already saddled with chores around the farm, but when Dad went to the hospital, they kicked (or were kicked) into third gear. They set the pace for the rest of us. On top of their normal chores, they added more chores, and went into town and got newspaper routes. Evening or morning routes, it didn't matter. From then on, they made their own spending money and added to the family coffers where they could.

This was the example Tom and I grew into, and were expected to follow.

At about the age of 10, it started with an afternoon paper route. Tom had doubled his route and I would help him. I had learned how to ride a bike so a hand-me-down from above was my method of transportation. A basket in front carried the newspapers. After a year as a helper, I got my own route. Now I was in business for myself, going door to door at the end of the month to collect pay for the month's newspapers.

When I was about 10, Dad got me a another part time, temporary summer job as a helper to an old friend of his, who worked for the Soil Conservation Service. I probably made 25 cents an hour, a good wage. For a 10-year-old kid, this was an exciting job. The Federal Government had imposed crop limitations on those farmers receiving government farm subsidies. Our crop of interest was peanuts, which abounded in the river bottom lands of the Arkansas River, about 10 miles away. Apparently, the market was over saturated. Using rods and a chain, we had to measure acreage planted in peanuts. If a farmer had more than his acreage allotment planted, he had to plow them up. Several times that summer, we were run off land by a farmer toting a shotgun, and we had to get assistance from the county sheriff. We always walked on to a farm, using the third biggest lie: "We are from the government, and we're here to help you." It didn't always work.

The paper routes continued until the age of 15, when I got my first "real" job. The summer after the ninth grade, I lied about my age (needed to be 16) and got a job across the road at Braden Winch company, which had bought the old CCC camp and started manufacturing all sizes of winches, and learned to run a drill press, punching holes in winch components. I had an arrangement to continue working part time after school started but that fell through because of the economy. So, it was back to delivering papers.

In the summer of 1950, I found a job on a road construction gang. We were building a new highway from Broken Arrow to Coweta, about 15 miles. It got so hot that summer that I had a light sunstroke in August and had to quit before school started. So it was back to delivering papers.

The next spring, classmates Lonnie Graham, Glenn Cone and I went into business. Glenn's mom bankrolled him and he bought an old junker flatbed truck. We hauled hay. We got paid by the bail for picking it up in the fields, and stacking it in barns. That was hard, hot work, but as we said, a good conditioner for football. I also had a minor accident on that job. The three of us were trying to move a tractor-pulled hay rake so we could get the truck closer to the barn. It got away from us and when the dust settled, one of the long, curved rake prongs was sticking half-way through my arm. I guess it was this job and the road gang that convinced me that I needed to get an education, as I surely didn't want to do those kind of things the rest of my life.

Glenn and Lonnie didn't see much future to hay hauling either, and our business was short term. Glen went on the road with some kind of a construction crew that required him to travel. He wrote back once, saying he was making so much money, that he might not be back for the Fall.

About halfway through the summer, I got a better job and left the hay hauling business. It was in a factory in Sand Springs, about 30 miles from home. I worked most of the summer on the night shift. The problem was I didn't have any transportation.

I remembered a fellow I knew at Braden Winch who lived in Tulsa. When he got off work in the afternoon, I rode with him to his house in Tulsa, then walked about 10 blocks through a bad part of town. There, I caught the Sand Springs trolley and rode to the plant. After work, when I got off at midnight, I reversed it, catching the last trolley back to Tulsa, walked those same 10 blocks (that was really scary) and climbed into the back seat of his car and went to sleep. When he arrived at Braden Winch for work in the morning, he woke me up and I walked home, slept until noon then repeated the trip in the afternoon. It made a long day, but that's the way the summer went. After about three weeks of this, I transferred to the day shift, and rode with another school boy who was working there.

When school started, it was back to the newspaper business. Now, however, we had the whole town, kind of as a manager, and I did all the legwork for Mom, i.e. finding and training carriers, collecting from them, etc.

The next summer, after I graduated from high school, I had a different kind of job. I was hired full time to be a yard caretaker for a family in Tulsa. I mowed, weeded, planted flowers, trimmed hedges, and took the lady of the house to the grocery store occasionally. That kept me busy all summer then I started to college.

We had all known that we would have to help pay the college expenses, and it was no different for me. I had the war bonds that I had saved through the war, and had been awarded a $300 scholarship from the Tulsa Tribune. My first year, I had a part time job in the University Press, working in the book bindery. On Saturdays, during the fall, after I had dropped out of the OU marching band, I sold cushions at the stadium during home football games.

The next summer I returned to Tulsa, and worked in Spartan Aircraft Corp in the parts department. They were rebuilding old military aircraft engines.

In the fall, back at OU, I worked in the fraternity house kitchen for meals, and also in the recreation center of the student union, racking pool tables. That fall was the first time I got paid for writing. A half dozen of us journalism students worked for the Daily Oklahoman sports desk on Thursday and Friday nights providing complete coverage on state high school football and basketball. The Daily Oklahoman bragged about covering every high school football game in the state. I continued to do this for the next three years.

The next summer, I worked in the machine shop of an oil field equipment manufacturer in Tulsa. My Uncle Joe helped me get this job. This was the company he had gone to work in at the age of 15, sweeping floors.

During my junior year, I had five different paying jobs. In retrospect, I wonder when I went to school, but there always seemed to be enough time. Two of these were part of the journalism curriculum, and included news editor of the Oklahoma Daily during the fall semester, and sports editor in the spring semester. These were extra-curricular activities, and we were graded; and fortunately, were paid. I was also a stringer for United Press International and provided sports coverage for most home events. I also had a job in the OU sports publicity office, writing sports press releases. My claim to fame was providing press coverage of the NCAA wrestling tournament held at OU to several state newspapers.

During the next summer before my senior year, I realized that I would not graduate on time without a summer school of picking up some credit hours and grade points. Mom had received a letter from the university, stating with regret that I would not graduate with my class. After garnering nine hours of A in summer school, I stayed at OU after the session was out, and worked in an amusement park during the day and at the Daily Oklahoman on the sports desk at night.

Then I began my senior year. The nine hours of A got me on the Dean's Honor Roll for the semester, but I was still on scholastic probation. Back when I was a freshman, I had auditioned for the OU marching band, the Pride of Oklahoma, and was selected. I had asked to be excused for the first football game because Tom, now an ensign in the Navy, was headed to Korea on an LST and this was his last weekend at home. I had wanted to spend some time with him. The band director told me, "If you're not here, quit band." So I quit band. I had enrolled in band for one hour credit, but failed to do the withdrawal paperwork. I ended the semester with one hour of F in band. Now, as a senior, I was able to get that changed to a withdrawal passing. That got me off scholastic probation list.

That's when I met my wife-to-be. During the first semester, I had a reporter's job in the Norman bureau of the Daily Oklahoman. There were only two of us, and we took pictures, wrote stories, and ran the teletype. It was probably one of the most enjoyable jobs I've ever had. I also worked in the kitchen of a boarding house for my meals. I had to pay for the additional expense of wedding rings. In the spring, I got a promotion--or at least recognition for the job I had done. I went to work full time at night, writing features for the Oklahoma City Times. I commuted back and forth between Norman and Oklahoma City every day.

I graduated that spring; married Mary Kathryn and we lived in Oklahoma City. I continued to work at the Oklahoma City Times as a full-fledged reporter until August, when I entered the Navy. I was supposed to return to the Times in 1959 when I would have gotten out of the Navy, but that didn't happen.

I had a lot of jobs growing up, and I did a lot of different things. Certainly, the best part of them was the money, for without it, I would never have completed school. There were also many intangibles. They helped me develop a sense of responsibility, something that I didn't have in earlier years. I learned a lot about what I didn't want to be when I grew up. I also learned a great deal about the kind of person I could be. So, all in all, the world of work was a tremendous part of my education, as well as providing the financial base to complete my formal education.

I guess the neat thing about it is that I always found time to study, had time for ample social life, courted bride to be, and had enough time to enjoy being a high school and college student.

The Club

This is about people with whom my three older brothers had a long and good relationship. I would have too, except I was a little later coming along, and only got to enjoy that adult relationship for a short time.

Marguerite Southwood (Maggie) was Mom's sister and her husband was Henry (Uncle Newt). In his younger years, Newt was a bantam weight boxer, and had all the potential to be a champion. But sometime in the 1920's, he contracted polio and spent the rest of his life in leg braces and walking with two canes.

Like Uncle Joe, they lived in North Tulsa, on Latimer, just off Denver in an apartment. It seemed like they always lived there, and probably did. They had two sons, Hank and Pat, a couple of years older than Mike and Bill. Pat was killed in Germany just before WWII ended. When Pat was brought home after the war, I was proud to be an altar boy at his funeral service. Hank spent about 35 years in the Army before retirement. He retired and lived in Lawton, Okla., until his death in 1989.

Newt and Maggie were fantastic people. They seldom went out but were tremendous hosts. Maggie was a jolly, heavy lady, who had such a good laugh and a tremendous sense of humor. I remember one time when she sold real estate, I helped her one night after dark put up "For Sale" signs in front of three new listings. She found out the next day we had placed them in front of the wrong houses. She laughed about that for years. Newt had a dry, and sometimes caustic sense of humor, and was a man of few words. He did like to listen to baseball games and the

Saturday night fights. I could watch his eyes and tell he was thinking of the way it could have been.

It was great to spend an evening with them. Drink a beer, play cribbage, gin rummy, or pinochle. I never got into the latter game, but sure enjoyed the first two. My brothers nicknamed their apartment "The Club." We were always invited to come by any evening, without even calling first, for a game of cards. Tom took advantage of this, but when I got to that age, there wasn't much time left.

The Club was a great place to take a date. Maggie and Newt could show her a good time. If she didn't play cards, they would have her wanting to learn. For awhile, when I was a freshman in college, I dated a girl who lived about three blocks away, and we spent a lot of evenings there. They had a doctor friend, Doc Jones, an osteopath, who was single, and a big red-headed Irish lush. He seemed to always be there with his girlfriend, Mildred.

There was a time in high school when I went roller skating one night in Tulsa with a group of kids. Gale Bart, a classmate of mine, got his feet tangled up with those of two other guys and they all fell. Gale got kicked in the mouth, which left a bad cut. I called Maggie, and by the time we got there, Doc had arrived and stitched up Gale at the dining room table.

During my freshman year in college, Newt became sick. He was in a very confused state of mind, and had only occasional periods of full alertness. Alzheimer's had not yet been identified so I don't know what it was called. He was placed in a nursing home in Oklahoma City, and occasionally, on Sunday, I would borrow a car, and come up from Norman and visit him. I would take him out for a drive, get an ice cream cone and take him back. He was always anxious for me, or anyone else, to leave, because he thought something bad would happen. He was never the same again.

Maggie kept The Club open, and it was always nice to come home from school over a weekend, have a date, and sometime during the evening, drop by Maggie's.

Within months after Mom contracted cancer, Maggie came down with the same type of cancer. While Mom was fighting through that five year recovery period, she watched Maggie die an agonizing death, a little bit each day. We saw her in 1966 when we were on our way to Washington. She was a shell of what she used to be, but never gave up that jolly laugh and the twinkle in her eyes.

With her death, The Club closed, for Maggie was "The Club."

Fundraising

School budgets were bare-bones during these times, like they are today. It seemed that the system was funded by auto license sales, and there didn't seem to be enough vehicles in Broken Arrow or Tulsa County. Parents and local merchants were outgoing in their support of schools, and various fundraising programs. There always seemed to be a fundraiser in progress for band uniforms and instruments. An auto dealer donated a car for the driver-training program. Students paid for their own books and supplies, and teachers, like today, spent personal money on supplies. The high school had its own programs for raising money for specific projects.

The state high school athletic system had very strict rules about gifts to student athletes. Only one gift over a certain dollar value could be given to a student. That was normally a letter jacket. For the second and third year of lettering, the student paid for his jacket. Broken Arrow High School had a unique system for raising money to buy football letter jackets for first-year lettermen. This system also provided for selecting a football queen. Other schools had similar systems for fundraising projects. Our system took away the privilege of the team voting on a candidate.

Each class, grades 9-12, nominated a candidate. That was by majority vote of each class. Then, each class had to raise money to support that candidate. The class that raised the most money in a given period of time (usually three to four weeks) presented its candidate as football queen, and whether she was the team favorite or not, she was crowned football queen. She usually got a full-page picture in the yearbook.

The money raised was used to buy letter jackets for the new lettermen on the football team. They didn't cost the school, or the athletic department, a penny. So, in that respect, it was good. Athletes got the honor they deserved, wore their jackets for a week or so, passed it on to their girlfriend, and the school never got a bill.

Money was raised by each class by any number of methods. There were bake and candy sales before school, noon and after school, carnivals in the gym, and raffles of anything we could get donated to raise money. In one of my classes, junior or senior--I can't remember which -- we had a gal who ran a kissing booth at our carnival.

Like most school-minded communities, Broken Arrow businesses were fully supportive of these fund raising events. Most all chipped in to buy chances, and help in other ways.

Our class never had a football queen. When we were seniors, and should have won, our queen candidate was Jean Blythe. We had all sorts of fun ways of raising money, and we were running well ahead with only a few days to go. We thought we had it locked up. Then, in the last days, the father, or uncle, of Margaret Wilson, the junior candidate, donated a side of beef to the junior class for a raffle, and they walked away with it with a narrow margin.

I have said before that we were all poor, but didn't know it. That was the feeling among everyone. But it wasn't always true. There were some folks who were less poor than others, and the junior class had them that year. One could say they bought the election--at least that's how we felt. On the other hand, Margaret Wilson was a pretty girl who was liked by everyone, and represented the B.A. Tigers well in her reign as football queen. It could have been just sour grapes on our part that we went through four high school years and never had a football queen. Jean was just as pretty, just as nice, and was just as popular.

Another popular fundraising program used in the high school system was Junior Work Day. This was a spring function sponsored by the junior class to raise money for some special project. We always seemed to have the necessities in school, but there were never many of the extras.

Junior Work Day was much like the "hire a slave" programs youth groups, athletic teams, and schools have today. It was a date on the school calendar in the spring semester. Juniors could get out of school on that date if they had a job, and the earnings for that day came into the school.

The town merchants were always quick to respond to this effort by creating one-day jobs for students. It was a race to get the best job we could. Students had to work at least four hours. I got a job at the American Legion Hut, racking balls on the pool tables. The owner had always been a big supporter of school programs, so he was happy to hire me. We shot pool in there frequently, so that's why I went to him. I was paid about 75 cents an hour, and worked all day. I was proud to turn in the money.

Mrs. Kennedy, our class sponsor, would not accept it. She was overly influenced by the purest religious thinking that money coming out of a pool hall where beer was served was somewhat tainted and a boy my age should not be in there. I conceded that she may be right, but since it had already happened, and we had the money, let's use it.

It upset me, because he had been such a good contributor to band, football and other school needs. No one hesitated in taking his money in those cases. I felt I had to return his money, and I did. I probably should not have. He became angry about it. "If my money is no good, then tell the school never to ask for another donation," was his attitude.

The school lost a good supporter--at least for a while. Eventually, he came back into the fold, I suppose, because of pressure from other merchants. I had a lot of respect for Mrs. Kennedy. She was one of four people outside of the family who had the greatest influence on my life. But, she blew it that time, I thought, and I lost a little of that respect.

Rudy

We always had at least one, and more often than not, two dogs at home. It just wouldn't have been a farm without an "Ol' Shep" around. We grew up reading the heroics of Lassie, Rin Tin Tin, and Call of the Wild and we had our own versions.

Dogs never came into our house. Inside was for people. They had their choice of two barns, but most of the time slept at the back door. During the winter, or one of those summer thunderstorms, the dogs would find a bale of hay in the barn. Buying dog food was unheard of. They ate scraps from the table. There was always a cat or two that lived in the barn—always at the whim of the dogs. Unlike the dogs, cats were not pets. They were barn animals and their sole purpose was to keep the mouse population in check.

In the true sense of the word, our dogs were never watch dogs. But in another sense, they were. They kept stray dogs out, and were protective of their territory—and we needed that. With chickens, cows and sheep, a stray dog, or even worse, a coyote coming on the property could cause havoc. In addition to our dogs, Dad always kept a loaded shotgun on the back porch to deal with a coyote.

Rudy is the dog I remember most. He was a mixed breed Collie that we got as a pup, when I was about 13. Rudy was Mary's dog, but we both shared him. He could have been Lassie's pup. At that time, we had downsized to a one-dog family, except for the times we boarded Andy, Uncle Horace's dog. Tom was away in college, and Mary and I were the only ones home. When we went to school, Rudy went to school; and that became his second home. He would sleep under the steps of the band room, an old WWII barracks building which had been moved to the school. He would return home with the first one to leave school. Rudy liked to play, liked to run, and liked to be around kids. Kids were at school.

When Mary would saddle up Pete, her horse, Rudy would wait patiently for a long run down the road or through the pasture. For some reason, he never wanted to follow me as I delivered my paper route on a bike. He had no interest in bikes.

Kirkland Field, the football field just across the road, became his running ground, even though we had 18 acres of pasture. There were seldom kids in the pasture. At a football game, he would go out with the team captains for the coin toss, and occasionally get excited and run onto the field during a game. Rudy ran regularly when the marching band practiced. He was always an unofficial part of half time marching routines. Through and around the ranks he would run, barking, but never upsetting the halftime routine.

It was not uncommon for the referees to stop the game to get Rudy off the field. For some reason, Rudy did not like officials. He would often bark at them, and occasionally chase the yellow flag when a ref threw it. I think the striped black and white shirts bothered him. When Coach was flagged with a delay of game penalty because of Rudy, things changed. Mary had to keep Rudy on a leash at the band bleachers. From then on, he would sit under the bleachers, tied to an iron post. Halftime was his game. When let free to run he would lead the band down the field. Occasionally, he was accepted by the visiting band.

When we had an away game, Rudy would be there waiting when the buses returned.

Rudy was a fixture at school. During class breaks, with students traveling between buildings--we had about six--Rudy was always there to be petted or played with. A look through my senior year book in the section containing candid pictures would reveal that Rudy was there more than I. After I graduated, Rudy had two more years to run and play at the high school with Mary and everyone else. He was there every day.

Finally, Mary graduated and took a job in Tulsa. Rudy would

spend the day wandering around the campus looking for her. When she arrived home in the evenings, Rudy was there to meet her.

A year after that, Mom sold the farm, Mary sold Pete, and Mom, Mary and Rudy moved to a neighborhood in Tulsa. Rudy's days of marching with the band, barking at football officials and disrupting a game, and running with Mary and Pete were over. Transitioning to a house/backyard dog over the next year was difficult.

Television In Broken Arrow

Today, television is a way of life. Whether it is good or not depends on how we use it, and to the degree we get addicted to it. It is common to have a 55-60-inch flat color set in the living room or den, 24-inch sets in the bedrooms and a smaller set in the kitchen. We stream movies through our computers, and can even watch them on our telephones, all received by WiFi, brought into the home by an underground cable or through the air from a satellite. If we miss a program, not to worry. It has been recorded and we'll watch it some other time. By the time this is published, there will be other innovations unheard of at this writing.

It hasn't always been this way. Television made its debut in the 1940s, or perhaps the late 1930s on an experimental basis. We first saw black and white TV in Broken Arrow in about 1951 when I was 16. On a small green screen, it featured lots of horizontal and sometimes vertical lines. Up to that time, and even for two or three years later, we continued to gather around the radio to just listen to our favorite programs.

We had heard about TV. There was a station in Oklahoma City, 120 miles away, that went on the air that year. This was big-time stuff, as we read about it in the newspapers and heard less about it on the radio. There was nothing to offer from Tulsa, the second largest city in the state. I didn't know of anyone who had a television set in Broken Arrow.

Mr. Smith had a shoe repair shop on Main Street. It was in an old 2-story building, as all of them were, that had a lot of glass frontage. He could make any old pair of shoes look like new, and would show them off in one of the windows. He used one pair to show the "before" and "after." The two shoes got a lot of attention. To attract new business, he bought a TV set, installed a wire frame antenna on the roof, and placed the TV in one of his big windows so that all could see. This turned out to be a successful marketing ploy. Everything was black and white--no color. The set had about a 14-inch screen, in a big vacuum tube cabinet, and the big antenna on roof of the second floor of his store to bring in the Oklahoma City channel.

He left the TV on at night. I remember going down town at night to stand with the crowd in front of his store window to watch whatever programming there was, which wasn't much, and the test pattern. At night, the National Anthem would play, the screen would go blank and the remaining watchers would go home. The test pattern was a series of vertical lines with criss-crossing horizontal lines. It would help the owner adjust the rotation of his antenna to bring in the best picture. In later years I remember lying on the roof, hearing "Turn it a little to the left . . . a little more . . . oops, too much, turn it back to the right." During these gyrations, the picture would rotate up or down, or completely disappear until the antenna was in the right position. When color came along, the test pattern was the big peacock with the array of rainbow colors in his tail feathers. The set owner could use that to adjust the color.

I stood there on the sidewalk many nights watching test pattern lines--usually among a lot of "snow," since the station was 120 miles away, until the station went off the air playing the National Anthem. As I would ride my bike home, I wondered if it would ever be popular.

The previous fall, Willard Fox, in a class ahead of me, made All-State at quarterback, and the All-State football game was to be televised by the Oklahoma City channel that spring. We stood there, watching mostly silhouettes with numbers we couldn't read. We couldn't distinguish between north and south jerseys and couldn't make out Willard, even though we knew his number, or anyone else for that matter, but we watched the game. We were mesmerized by the picture on the screen, but the old timers said it would never be popular. They were wrong about that. The next year, Tulsa had its own station and rooftop antennas began to proliferate the neighborhoods. I could always tell who had TVs from the antennas. We never had a TV in our home in Broken Arrow because they were so expensive.

The next time I saw television was in the fall of 1952, when I went to college at the University of Oklahoma. The fraternity had a big console in the fraternity house. That was high class. Living in the dorm, I would come all the way to the house after class to watch such things as Yogi Bear and the McCarthy hearings in Congress. Sitting around watching television with a bunch of fraternity brothers was an atmosphere of confusion. There were only two channels and someone always wanted to watch the other channel. It was get up and change the channel. Then get up and change it back. Not long after that, a remote was invented that could change the channel from the couch. But a wire connected it to the TV. People walking through the room would trip over the wire, or someone would catch it in the vacuum cleaner. Now, the wire is gone and it is really done remotely.

How much our lives have been changed by "the tube."

Shelby - - What Is Education?

Mrs. Kennedy, our junior English teacher, was furious. It was time to study literature, and she had assigned weekend homework concerning the poets Shelly and Keats.

She called on Shelby Smith to answer questions. He couldn't. She told him in no uncertain terms that if he didn't do his homework, he would fail. Shelby was the son of a farmer. No one really considered Shelby too smart. But that day, he was brilliant. He did a job on Mrs. Kennedy.

In response to his failure notification, Shelby rose and addressed Mrs. Kennedy, the class, and the world.

"Miz Kennedy," he said in his country voice, "I had two choices this weekend: Fix the John Deere tractor or study about Shelly and Keats. Now, if I don't fix the tractor, we don't get the crops in, we don't make any money, and we end up short of food for the winter. I think Shelly and Keats care less whether I study about them or not, and sure enough, if I do, it won't help put food on the table this winter. So, Miz Kennedy, I chose to work on the tractor."

"Miz Kennedy," he continued, "Do you know how to fix a John Deere tractor when it breaks?"

"No" was the response.

"I do," he replied. "But it took most of the weekend. And now, we have it back in the field."

He had made his point.

In his 50s, Shelby was still farming, after inheriting the land his parents farmed years ago. Considering the farm crisis as it presently is,

Shelby is about as successful as the next farmer. I'm not sure, but he probably had another job in town to supplement his income.

Miz Kennedy, in her 70s, is retired, and is very ill physically, at this writing. Her mind is as sharp as a tack, and she has some very strong words about education. "Why is it," she says, "that our education system feels the need to teach kids the value of formal education, but does not help them learn to make a living?" I'm sure she was thinking of the many Shelby Smith's she had taught over the years--with a curriculum mandated by the state--which did Shelby, for the most part, little good.

Shelby is still farming--a career choice. Mrs. Kennedy never learned to fix a tractor.

The Junior-Senior Fight

That's just what it was--a fight. It had been a traditional spring event in Broken Arrow for many years. I remember Mike, Bill and Tom all participating in it in previous years. Now, I was a junior and it was our turn.

It may have once been a school sponsored event, but by 1951 when I was a junior, it had dwindled to the point of "under-the-table" sanction because the school was backing away from overt sponsorship.

The fight always occurred in the spring--usually in the last six weeks of school. The rules were simple. The junior class went out in the country and put up a flag--in a tree or on a pole.

The senior class had to take it down as the juniors defended. It officially started at sundown, and ended at sunrise, if not earlier. There was always a bonfire, lots of grease on the pole, pop--and sometimes beer--to drink. The girls--those who could get out--came and watched, and they too sometimes fought. Occasionally curious townspeople came out and observed.

The juniors set the date, and had to notify the seniors before the end of school on fight day. The seniors had to find the flag. There was a rule that if they didn't find it by a certain time, the juniors had to provide the location. That never was a problem since there were always ways of finding out.

The fight was the social event of the spring semester. It has been replaced over the years by such things as Spring Break, ski trips, and trips to Six Flags, which were all unheard of during those times. Our spring break was Good Friday off, if even that. Although social in nature, and a lot of fun, the fight was also something else. It was a time to officially settle any grudges developed during the year. Everyone--juniors and seniors alike--had someone in mind in the other class to "get."

Between the time the announcement was made and sundown, it wasn't safe to be alone around the school or on the downtown streets. We always traveled in twos, threes, and better still, fours. To be caught alone on the street by a group from the other class meant a trip 20 miles outside of town and left to walk back--barefooted at the minimum. Sometimes worse things happened. It was one way of eliminating some of the opposition. I was never involved in one of these excursions, either as the taker or takee, but I've watched them happen.

As I recall, the fight always ended on relatively friendly terms with most grudges settled. The settling of grudges was always secondary in purpose. Primary was defending the flag or taking in down. Somehow, in all that, the secondary purposes were satisfied too.

Occasionally, there was an accident and someone got hurt. Black eyes, bruises, bloody noses, skins and scrapes were not considered as being hurt. Such an accident had occurred when Tom was a senior. One of his classmates, while wearing telephone pole climbers, was pulled off the pole and someone at the bottom had his leg ripped open. This kind of thing, although rare, placed a bad reputation on the fight in some corners.

We got a new principal the year I was a junior. Norval Baldwin came all the way from Bixby, 14 miles away. The "bad reputation" had traveled that far. One of his first policy declarations was that there would be no junior-senior fight. It was over and done with, period. There would be no discussion. Little did he know. But the under-the-table sanction was gone.

As the first semester turned to the second, basketball turned to baseball, and winter turned to spring, whispers began to surface about the "fight." Mr. Baldwin restated his policy decision, but that seemed to fan the flames.

We decided to put the pole up in a back corner of Fred Dorrell's farm. We would do it first class. We had a long telephone pole, and we would use his farm equipment to dig the hole and cement it into the ground. We had about 100 pounds of oil rig grease to fully cover the pole. We would skip school one day, put the pole up, and have the fight two days later. There were about eight of us who skipped school that day--John Dale McCuistion, Lonnie Graham, Glenn Cone, Fred Dorrell and I, among a few others. We all had our own excuses and had phoned them into school. John Dale had to help his Dad and I had to take Tom back to Stillwater to school, etc. The only glitch was that about 11 a.m., John Dale's Dad needed him and came to school to pick him up. It didn't take Mr. Baldwin long to check on the rest of us, and he was smart enough to put 2 and 2 together. Somehow, they found out where we were. John Dale's dad and Mr. Baldwin arrived at Fred's farm, as we poured the cement: a beautiful, straight standing pole with a white skivvy shirt at the top. When we saw them coming, we all knew we were in trouble, especially John Dale. The rest of us scattered.

We were all in his office at 8 a.m. the next morning for a stern lecture and a severe warning. Two of the guys, because of previous problems, were suspended at the time. Another glitch developed. The word had gotten around, and Fred's brother, Val Gene, a senior, went home, found the pole, and pulled it down with a tractor.

Mr. Baldwin had another weapon to use in combating the fight: write to the parents. The letter he generated, signed by the superintendent, himself, and members of the Board of Education, was given to all students to take home to parents. In part, it read:

"The students are threatening bodily harm to the ones who do not participate in the fight. We believe an individual has the right to choose whether or not he takes part in this activity, and should not be punished if he does not participate. The school will definitely regulate the trouble this causes on the school campus or during classes. It is difficult for the school to regulate activities that take place at night or weekends. We assure you the Board of Education and the school administration will go with you 100 percent in regulating or stopping it."

Meanwhile, the word was out in school. Anyone getting caught doing anything connected with a junior-senior fight during school hours or on school property would be suspended immediately. We had to be careful.

I brought the letter home that night, and Mom and I discussed it. I assured Mom that everything would be all right, but it looked for certain that the fight would be toward the end of the week. I got her reluctant blessing to participate, but I said I would try to stay out of trouble at school.

The next night, we all met. Lonnie Graham knew of an old tree on some river bottom property where we could have it. It was on the farm next to his. The two that had been suspended spent the next day stripping the limbs, putting up a flag, and greasing the tree. We had decided the fight would be that Friday night.

It was my job to inform the senior class and get the word out to all juniors. In fights past, the notification was always put on the school bulletin boards. But under the new policy, we had to be more subtle. I was in English class that afternoon. Mrs. Willie Kennedy, my teacher, had as much influence on my growing up as anyone else. She was a real jewel. I was good in English and finished my assignment early. I had about 30 minutes left, and she said I could work on anything I wanted.

I guess I was too quiet--which was unusual, and that meant trouble--because I discovered her looking over my shoulder as I completed the last of three announcements which would be placed on bulletin boards during class break. They read similar to the following:

"The Junior Class invites the Senior Class to participate in a social gathering and get acquainted party tonight."

That's all that was needed to announce the fight. And her catching me was all that was needed to get me a trip to Mr. Baldwin's office. Fifteen minutes later, I was suspended for three weeks and on my way home. The announcements didn't get posted. They didn't have to be. Word went around the school in a flash.

One of the hardest things I ever had to do while growing up was to go home and tell my Mom that I had been suspended. It was tough and I was a big disappointment to her. When anything like that happens today, the parents would take the school system to court, but in those days, we took our lumps.

"We know we are living in a year of hysteria, unrest and anticipation," the letter continued. *"If there ever was a time when students need to settle down and get as much from their classes as possible, it is now. Leadership must be developed for the future. We don't think the Junior and Senior fight will help develop the kind of leadership needed."*

The fight was on. After being suspended, I don't know why Mom let me go, but she did. I guess I do know--it was just that important and she realized it.

I had two names on my grudge list--Jim Young and Marvin Apple. I guess I was on a couple of lists also, because it was a busy night.

The fight ended at sunrise, which meant the flag was still flying. We didn't have any Francis Scott Key's in our class so no song was written. It was the first time in many years the juniors had won.

It had been the custom in years past, when the fight had the school's under-the-table sanction, for the president of the winning class to present the flag to the losing president as part of Commencement exercises. We just didn't have the courage to do that. We did, however, get it to them.

I ended up getting back in school after about two weeks, after agreeing to all sorts of conditions of good behavior for the remainder of the year.

The following year, when I was a senior, the fight was held again. Many of the same kind of things happened, but there just didn't seem to be the spirit because Mr. Baldwin really clamped down. But we won again--the first class in years to win on both sides of the fight.

The next two years were Mary's junior and senior years, and the fight died after her senior year. The iron hand of Mr. Baldwin, who later became superintendent, dealt the death blow. That's probably when trips to Six Flags started.

It was a tradition lost.

Growing Up Too Early

G lenn Cone, a classmate of mine, was one of my idols in high school, and perhaps my best friend that year. I guess it is rather strange for one to have an idol who is the same age and same status, but he was that to me. He was such a tremendous athlete and always seemed so cool. We nailed down that friendship not long before when we were both suspended from school because of participation in the junior-senior fight. We spent a lot of time together those two weeks, often driving into Tulsa where we could shoot pool and get a beer where a buck on the counter sufficed for an ID.

At one time, Glenn and I were vying for the same girl friend, Iva Mae Cates. I tried to cut him out of the pattern but he won her heart and they were married some time after school. They were still happily married when he was killed in an auto accident some 30 years later.

Glenn and I were 17, and seniors, and we felt we had grown up. We had a good football year and recently, had beaten the seniors in the junior-senior fight. During that year, and the year before, we had spent a lot of our spare time shooting pool at the American Legion Hut. Jimmy, a toothless old reprobate who probably looked much older than his years, was caretaker of the pool tables. He was lord over a couple of snooker tables and two or three pool tables. He was the "Minnesota Fats" of Broken Arrow. He taught us everything we knew about shooting pool. I enjoyed listening to him tell stories about the good ol' days."

The owner of the Hut was a community minded person who never hesitated to support any activity connected with the school. It didn't make any difference whether it was band uniforms, football equipment, or books for the library, he was always first in line to donate. He who gave me a job racking balls during Junior Work Day. So, we always chose to play pool there. There was one other place in town, but we always went to the Hut, even though it was dark and dingy, and always smelled of stale smoke and beer and spittoons regularly used.

Glenn and I thought we had grown up. It was one of those things that happens frequently at that age, and somebody eventually would put us in our place. We walked into the Hut that hot afternoon, having already decided we'd have a beer before we played. We bellied up to the bar like we knew what we were doing, rolled the dice to see who was buying, and ordered a Falstaff.

The owner put us in our place. We weren't old enough.

We were embarrassed, angry and hurt. The macho image we presented crumbled around us. We left in a huff, and drove around, through the alley to the back door. I'm not sure just why, but I think we wanted to unobtrusively come in the back door and shoot our game of pool.

Lo and behold, there was a beer delivery truck parked in the back. Glenn looked at me with that mischievous grin, and said, "Hell, Connery, if they won't sell us one, we'll take one." He backed and filled to get my window (passenger side) alongside the open side bay of the truck. I reached out and in an instant, had a case of bottles sitting in my lap and we were gone.

We went to the park to have a brew. I looked through the glove box for a "church key." Our macho image had returned and we were cool. I got the case open and handed Glenn an empty bottle. I had pulled off a case of empties. I thought Glenn would kill me. But we had a good laugh.

We didn't want this failure to go down on our records so it was back to the Hut. The beer truck was still there. Glenn would do it this time, so he pulled alongside the open bay. Out the window the case of empties went, back into the slot. Glenn reached for a case of cans. His arm and hand were so big and strong that he lifted the case from the truck and pulled it into the window with one hand. I pulled it onto my lap and we were gone again.

Back to the park we went. One beer, especially when it was hot, was about all we could handle on a hot summer day. So after finishing one, we hid the case in his trunk under some work clothes. We would get back to it later. I had perhaps two more of the beers over the summer.

That spring, Glenn, Lonnie Graham and I went into the hay hauling business. Glenn's family had an old flatbed truck, and we would load it in the field then stack the hay in barns. After unloading the truck, we would have one of the remaining beers. It was a hot, dirty job, and I guess because of that, and a small accident I had, I decided there were easier ways of making money, and shortly after school was out, I found a job in a manufacturing plant in Sand Springs.

It was during that hay hauling experience that I met David, a Negro boy about my age. He was also working with a crew, composed of his dad and two others. David was my first contact with Negroes, the first one I had ever known personally. He lived just on the outskirts of the city limits on a small farm. Negroes could not live inside the town limits, or go to school in Broken Arrow. They could shop in town, but had to be out of town by sundown. Alsuma was a small black community between Broken Arrow and Tulsa. David went to school there.

I don't remember Lonnie or Glenn associating with David, but I wanted to, perhaps out of curiosity. I had seen Negroes in Broken Arrow on a Saturday but there had never been any contact. My contact with him in those short weeks was limited, just meeting once in a while in the hay fields. Once, when we happened to be there at the same time, we ate lunch together in the shade of his truck. I would liked to have known him better but there was never the opportunity.

Glenn and Lonnie didn't stay in the hay hauling business much longer either, perhaps for the same reasons. It could have been also because the truck carburetor had a problem with vapor locking. It was common to have it loaded, in the middle of a hay field, and not be able to get it started.

One day, Lonnie, Glenn and I and a couple of other guys were in the Hut shooting pool when Lonnie and Glenn got into a tiff over something. Words got a little louder and a little stronger until they decided to go out back and settle it. I had never seen them argue as they seemed to have been the best of friends for almost three years, but this time it was serious. I didn't go out with them as I didn't want to see it - - my two friends fighting. Out they went. About 15 minutes later, Lonnie came back in, stating, "If ida thought I could do it, I woulda done it a long time ago." I did not see Glenn the rest of the day, but the next day he was sporting a real shiner. He and Lonnie were friends again.

Glenn got on with a construction crew that moved about a two or three state area. I got a letter from him, I presume in mid to late July, from somewhere out of state, and answered it, addressing him as "Big Wheel." (Wheel and Big Wheel were popular monikers of the day). Glenn was making the best money he had ever made and had hinted that he might not return for his senior year. Years later, after Glenn died, Iva Mae found my reply in his personal things and returned it to me. It is reproduced below. He must have indicated some concern that Bob Latch, a friend who had just graduated, was trying to get close to Iva Mae. He must have also said that if he didn't come back, I could have Iva Mae (as if she wouldn't have anything to say about it).

I have chosen to include this letter for a number of reasons. First of all, it is included because of the language. A boy that age had to keep up his "big wheel" (now macho) image. The way to do that, we thought, was to use profanity liberally. That's not too different today, even with girls. Secondly, it is such a fantastic reminder of a part of growing up, the things we did, the things we thought important. I am embarrassed about the words used, and the penmanship. Each time I read it now in completing this book, it triggers something else—another memory.

The most important reason, however, is that Glenn chose to keep it all these years. That really means a lot to me. I wish he were here now so I could tell him that. I have wondered why it would be that important to him? Certainly, it had to be an ego builder to him. Glenn did not need that, however. Glenn was the "all-time cool." To compare him with someone you are familiar with, he would be close to the "Fonz" from Happy Days. Lastly, it shows that I didn't take penmanship lessons seriously.

Except for his football ability, not many people gave Glenn much credit. I think it was close to a consensus that he would not amount to much. Glenn, on the other hand, knew that whatever he did would turn out all right. He didn't have a whole lot of interest in school, and for the most part, was there for football, to be with friends, and because he was supposed to be. I think he was halfway serious about not coming back.

Perhaps it was my letter--a letter from a friend--that got him back in school that fall. Perhaps that's why he kept it. I would like to think so, but I don't know.

Glenn did come back that fall, made All-Conference in football, and graduated with me in 1952. I didn't come close to making the first team, but it was always important to me that he thought I could. Glenn went into the Army after high school, and was a paratrooper. Sometime during this period, he married Iva Mae, his high school sweetheart. When he got out, he went to Tulsa University and got his degree in accounting. When he graduated from TU, he sent announcements to the Broken Arrow principal, superintendent, and probably to some members of the Board of Education--the people who thought "he wouldn't amount to much." Lonnie went on to Northeastern Oklahoma Junior College and played football. On completion, he went on to Texas Tech where he played for two years, where he was nicknamed the "Lone Ranger" because he wore glasses and goggles over them when he played.

Glenn went on to be probably one of the most successful in our class, owning an oil production company and oil well servicing company at the time of his death in 1983. It was in the last three years of his life that we reestablished contact and continued a good friendship.

Friday Night

Big Wheel,

What the hell do you mean travelig all over hell and part of Texas just to wrk I don't give a damn how much you are making next August the 25th you better have your little ass here in B.A.U. If you think I'm going to play football if you are not here you are crazy as hell. If your not here who is going to raid beers truck with me. And as for Iva Mae. If I see Bob Smith messing around with her, I will stomp the fucking hell out of him. As for going with her if you don't come back, I don't see how I could fit into your shoes and be the kind of guy you are. I will do the best I can to take care of here for you and I know damn well she will be waiting for you.

If you think I can make all-conference and you say I can I know damn well I can but I want you here to make it with me.

Not much going on around here. Still raining like hell.

Well, hell, not much more to say so will close now. Send your new address with the next letter.

Take it easy or
any way you can get it —
John.

Matootin's Tooters

Late in our junior year, we felt the need for a dance band. I really don't recall why, because, as I remember, we were not allowed to dance, except at an occasional sock hop. The Baptist and Assembly of God influence on our school board and administration frowned on dancing. It would be more appropriate if we called it a swing band.

We formed one. John Dale McCuistion put it together. "Matootins Tooters," we called it. In earlier years, John Dale had a speech impediment and that's how he pronounced his named: Matootin. It was a small group--six pieces--and consisted of John Dale, leader and trombone; Bob Lemon, clarinet/saxophone; Mutt White and Dale Crowder, trumpets; Edna Tarleton, piano, and me on the drums. Occasionally, someone, boy or girl, would come out of the glee club and sing with us. We were seniors, except Dale Crowder and Bob Lemon, who were juniors. Dale was one of the guys who came in from Lynn Lane. After college, he became a Navy jet pilot, and was killed on a training mission, flying out of Hawaii, in about 1960. As I recall, he just disappeared off the radar scope and without any radio contact.

We never played for a dance, but we did get to play at a lot of functions, including school programs and civic group functions downtown. We got stage time on Main Street at Rooster Day and Cotton Day celebrations. We thought we were pretty good. We would take popular sheet music, and rearrange it to fit our style – and ability. We had taken Jane Metz's music theory course, where we, individually, had to write music, which was a big help to us. John Dale was the main writer/arranger. We had a lot of fun with it. Gesin had taught us how to read and play music--Jane Metz had taught us how to write and arrange, and we were off and running.

That year and a half gave me the experience necessary to play drums with various dance bands occasionally in college, which helped a little financially, until I found in my last two years that I could make more money writing.

Mary and Mom, 1950

Mary and I, 1951

The High School

Hut Hut Hut

Matootin's Tooters: John Dale
McCuistion, Bob Lemon, Edna
Tarleton, Mutt White, Dale
Crowder and me

The Fearsome: Standing L/R: Glenn
Cone, Lonnie Graham, Charles
Chenoweth, John Dale McCuistion,
Ed Schoeffler; In Front: me, Dwayne
Barrett, Art Davis, Tom Dotson

Braces Unnecessary

The Connery family, through heredity, had a problem with protruding and crooked teeth. It came from my mother's side, the Eustice clan. I was the only one of the five in my family who had the problem, but I have seen it in following generations. When I was about 13, I had to go to the dentist to get a tooth filled. By this time, we were using Dr. Spann, who was new in town, and a good dentist; and besides that, he didn't play religious music or preach to us.

He did suggest to Mom that she take me to an orthodontist. We didn't know what that was, so he told us. We got an appointment with one in Tulsa and went--and we found out it would cost about $500 for braces to straighten my teeth. My mother laughed. There was just no way we could come up with that kind of money, so the issue was dropped. To my favor, it was not much in vogue to be a "metal mouth." However, three of my offspring have worn braces, and were never ostracized socially because of it. They were kind of like a badge of honor.

The pain of braces and that expense would have been a waste of money and time for Mom and me. One football scrimmage my senior year, I was playing opposite Glenn Cone. On one play, he caught me across the mouth with an elbow block which rang my bell. Rarely did anyone wear a faceguard then. My mouth hurt for days, my front teeth were loose, and I lost weight on a liquid diet. I was careful during the rest of the year about what I ate - - drank lots of malts and milkshakes. I was careful about what I said - - I talked funny. I knew how Mutt White felt a year ago.

About two months before graduation, my front teeth started to turn dark. The dentist said that the hit had killed all the nerves in three of them. We went back to Dr. Spann and he said all four of my upper front teeth would all have to come out. There were molds taken, measurements made, etc. and a temporary plate made.

We were nearing graduation, and I wanted to have this completed by that time. In the meantime, we had been planning a senior prom, the first ever acknowleged, but not sponsored by the school. It would be held at the Mayo Hotel in Tulsa, the grand old hotel of the oil boom. I hadn't arranged a date because I didn't know what my mouth would look like. Dr. Spann assured me that I would look all right even though suffering some discomfort. At the last minute, I got a date with Alice Mahaffey, a junior who played drums with me in the band. We had been good friends for the past two years but had never dated. Other than friendship, there was no attraction between us. I just needed a last minute date and I'm sure she said "yes" just so she would be included at the event.

On the day of the prom, I went to school that morning, then to the dentist that afternoon, had four teeth pulled, the temporary inserted, then picked up Alice that night with four new front teeth. They were neat and straight, and my gums bled all evening, but nobody noticed. It was the prom. I didn't need braces after all. When I said goodnight to Alice that night, I did not try to kiss her. It would have hurt too much.

Who Wants Panties?

Toward the end of our senior year, and most of us had lined up our immediate plans for the future. There were a few of us who were going to college (OU, Oklahoma A&M, TU and others). Some had football scholarships; many were going right to work--in factories, offices, businesses and a few back to the farm. Some would be going in the service.

There were four of us going to the University of Oklahoma. We would be Sooners: Charles Chenoweth had an NROTC scholarship; Bob Smith, hoping one day to be a doctor; Carl Clayton; my roommate, and me, to be a famous journalist. There were as many going to a number of other places. Since we were such a small community, most people who were involved in school knew where everybody was going.

That spring, college campus riots, or close to that, erupted across the nation in the form of panty raids. It was one of those fads that lasted a year. The year before, it was something like how many students could get into a phone booth, or a Volkswagen. The University of Oklahoma got nationwide publicity on its panty raids that spring. These raids had to do with the guys racing through girls' dorms, stealing panties; or the girls throwing panties out windows to the guys, while campus security people and local police tried to disperse the crowd of curious onlookers.

We heard about all that in Broken Arrow. The Tulsa newspapers had coverage every day, and those who now had television saw it in the once-a-day news. Some students were arrested, some were suspended from school, and others got their panties. Sin had truly come down upon our campus. Parents fretted about sending their children off to that kind of environment. The week of high school graduation, an editorial charge in the Broken Arrow Ledger, addressed to the four of us, read something like the following:

"To our children going to OU. If you feel you need a pair of panties, please don't go down to Norman and engage in that kind of unruly conduct. Don't embarrass yourselves, your school, your town and your parents. Just drop by our office and we'll give you a pair."

None of the four of us felt the need to have a pair of panties, so we didn't take them up on their offer. When I went to OU that fall, panty raids were a thing of the past. Something else had replaced them. Besides that, it was football season and Bud Wilkinson's Sooners would be No. 1 in the country, while Dr. George Cross, president of the university, worked on making the school "something the football team could be proud of."

My Love Life

Boys and girls meeting each other in the age of awareness is a big part of growing up. Attractions are developed, and soon, one is going "steady," completely enamored by the one of the opposite sex.

I missed the boat somewhere. That never happened with me in high school. It was truly the "age of innocence" for me. I don't know the reason, but I would like to believe it was because I was a late bloomer. In fact, it was just being scared.

As you have read, there was Gwilda in the first grade, but she moved. In the third, Suzanne didn't appreciate the rubber ball, and that ended that. I guess I then took a sabbatical for the next few years. My experience the first year at scout camp did not help. The time later when I carried a rubber, got caught and punished did not ring any bells about sex.

In high school, I dated a number of girls at different times, some of whom I have seen in later years at reunions, and they remain good friends. There was never anything more than a "crush," in which a date ended with, at most, a kiss good night at the front door. As I look back now, the only real and serious attraction I had was to a girl already taken--by my best friend. Perhaps I let myself develop that attraction because I knew she wasn't available. Meanwhile, there were several different parking spots along country roads that my buddies used.

Having a "steady" was almost a social requirement in the upper two grades of high school. One needed someone to wear his football jacket. If you didn't have a girl, you could get along, but it was a lot tougher. Some went from steady to steady, and others got married after graduation and are still married 60 plus years later. It was always fun to watch, after sports letter jackets were awarded, how long the boy kept it before losing it to some girl.

My first exposure to sex was when, at the age of 16, my friend and I were taken by his boss to a whore house on First Street in Tulsa. He wanted to make "men" of us. I went into that experience very frightened, and had a very difficult time going up the steps, but because of peer pressure, I couldn't back out. I came away from that experience feeling like Peggy Lee, when she sings the song, "Is that all there is?" My next sexual experience, believe it or not, was with my wife six years later, the night we were married.

Until that time, in retrospect, it seems that any incident where touching or the removal of clothing was involved, memories of that night at the scout camp returned and the resultant fears put a damper on things.

There were a couple of hot courting sessions, one in high school and one in college, which led to invitations to stay, but I managed to "escape."

The summer I graduated from high school, my brother Bill and family lived in the barn apartment. Bill sold life insurance and he had a young lady client, whose husband had been killed in a truck wreck. Carolyn was a year or two older than me and her husband had been in Tom's class. I had known her before her marriage as she worked the morning shift at a local restaurant and I would often stop by there for coffee after delivering my paper route. That summer, she came to the house a couple of times after work in the evening in settlement of a life insurance policy. Bill and Carolyn would sit in the back-yard glider and discuss business. I joined them one evening just to say hello. I sat next to her, and after about 20 minutes, she grabbed my hand. It sent electric shock waves through my entire body. I dated her only a couple of times until Mom found out. Mom did not want me dating Carolyn. "She's had a husband and she will expect more from you than you're willing to give," she lectured. So, I didn't date Carolyn. But that was the closest to a sexual lecture I ever received from either of my parents, including the rubber incident. After I had started at OU, I fanatisized about having Caroline down for a weekend, but that never happened. I dated a lot in college, but those dates were never more serious than those I had in high school, except for one: Late in my sophomore year, I was "pinned" to Liz Flinn, a girl from Tulsa. Being pinned meant that she wore my fraternity pin and was a little stronger commitment than going steady. For a while, we were going to "conquer the world." That broke up in my junior year, but we remained friends throughout the years until her death.

I dated other girls that junior year, but those dates were all casual. Then, as a senior in the fall of 1955, I met my future wife, Mary Kathryn, and we were married the next year.

Dropping OU Band

I was a good drummer, perhaps not as good as my brother Bill, but I never admitted that to anyone. I had played drums since the seventh grade and now was a freshman at the University of Oklahoma.

The previous spring, our high school band had been down to OU for one of the Spring band contests, and Gesin arranged an audition for me with the OU band director. The audition went well. I thought I had drummed well for him until he asked me to play a paradiddle and I didn't know what he was talking about. I found out later that a paradiddle was one of about 40 essential rudiments of good drumming. I knew most of them, but did not know the names. Nevertheless, he accepted me and I would be a member of the University of Oklahoma Marching Band, the Pride of Oklahoma. If you have seen them perform, or get a chance to see them on TV at a football game halftime, you'll know why they are called that. It is breathtaking to watch them march down the field in that interlocking OU formation.

I was proud. It was the Fall of 1952 and I was to be a part of the band that supported Bud Wilkinson's Oklahoma Sooners, who had won national championships in 1950 and 1951. Enrolled for one hour credit. I took my place in the band and we practiced, practiced, and practiced, then practiced some more. We spent about as much time on the field practicing as did the football team. And that didn't include the band room practice. Everything had to be perfect. There was a saying in the band room, mimicking a previous saying by the OU president, "We want a band that the team can be proud of."

Finally, it was time for the first OU football game, at home, against the University of Pittsburgh and we were ready to go. We were to appear in pre game ceremonies, as well as at halftime. I was excited.

Meanwhile, the previous spring, Tom had graduated from Oklahoma A&M (now Oklahoma State University) and had completed the remainder of his naval training, was commissioned an ensign, and came home on short notice for a weekend leave before going to catch a ship off the coast of Korea (that was the war then).

I was caught up short. To march at halftime in Owen Stadium in front of 50,000 people, or go home to see Tom before he left for war. I talked to the band director about getting off that weekend. He told me to "be there or drop band," and that he needed a decision because if I weren't to be there, he needed to fill a spot. Taking the game off and coming back next week just wasn't an alternative. He didn't have much empathy for the fact that my brother was going to war, and may not come back, as many others didn't.

In many ways, it was a tough decision to make. In other ways, it was easy. I went home to see Tom. The next week, I was no longer part of the Pride of Oklahoma. I had taken band for one hour of credit, but I didn't take the necessary steps to formally drop it. So, at the end of my first semester, I had one hour of F in band.

Four years later, when I was scrounging for grade points to graduate on time, I rediscovered that on my transcript. I went to the university, explained the situation, and petitioned to have that changed to "withdrawal passing." Fortunately, it was approved.

I stayed with music during my four years of college, occasionally playing with dance bands on weekends to earn an extra buck or two. In retrospect, I would now make the same decision, given the two choices I had. Tom was a lot more important to me than the band. However, every time I see that band on TV, or listen to my nephew Phil Connery talk about his experiences –he was in it three years -- I can't help but wish there could have been a way.

Luck Runs Out

In all the scrapes I had been through in the previous 10-12 years, including almost bleeding to death in my sleep, running into fences and through windows, teeth getting jarred loose, and a couple of car wrecks, I never had a broken bone. I must have been capable of taking brutal punishment.

Then I went to OU. The "tea sipper" school, they called it then, they being the Aggies (now OSU). Entering OU, having heard this label, I thought it would be a suave, debonair atmosphere, and I practiced all summer cocking that little finger and holding a teacup.

When I graduated from high school, I weighed about 160. When I entered OU, I weighed 185-190, the heaviest I have ever been. The first week I was there, I met Billy Vessels, Heisman trophy winner, and All-American Guard and Outland Trophy winner J.D. Roberts, who tipped the scales at about 210 pounds. They weren't so big. John Dale McCuistion weighed more than that, and I held my own with him at 160 in football scrimmages. For a short period of time, I had fantasies about being a walk-on and earning the big "O." I say a short period-- until I went out and watched practice the first time. None of that for me, so I continued practicing cocking my finger, and resigned myself to the fact that I would just write about football.

In the dorm, I was introduced to intramural flag football. C Dorm, Cross Center, part of a new men's dorm complex, was to have a football team. I had pledged Theta Kappa Phi, a Catholic fraternity, and they had a football team also. Since the Greeks played only Greeks, I got the opportunity to play for both teams.

Flag football sounded kind of tame for me, but it turned out to be pretty rough, since there were no pads. I found all the contact sport I wanted in these two leagues. The dorm team, all freshmen, consisted of a bunch of rowdies, whereas the fraternity team was "cool", yet good. I played linebacker for both teams--no use switching positions when switching teams. After the first week, we were 1-0 on both teams. The second week got tougher.

My dorm team played first that week, against a team that was rowdier than we were. I took a blind side block which flipped me over, and I came down on my right hand. Damn, it hurt. I went out for a while, put some ice on it, and came back in the fourth quarter. That game ended in a tie. Two days later, my fraternity team would play.

I soaked my hand and forearm that night. The next morning, my right wrist was twice as big as the left. I went to the infirmary and had it X-rayed. I had a broken bone in my wrist, which was a little out of place. After undue pain and torture, they got it back in place and I wore a cast for the first time ever. I often blamed that for my poor academic performance that year as it was so difficult to write. My instructors gave me few breaks.

I sat out the fraternity game that week, but was back the following games. My cast came just short of the elbow, and I could wrap it in foam rubber and play. Even wrapped and padded, I found it to be an effective weapon. I could go up with a pass receiver, come down over him with my arm to knock down the pass and rap him in the head and shoulder area. It never hurt them, but it got their attention. The next time one was out for a pass, he knew what was going to happen, thus his full concentration was not on catching the ball.

Soon, the intramural season was over, but I still had a cast. By that time, my wrist had started to itch. I would often stick a pencil down in the cast to scratch. The more I scratched, the more it itched. And I could never find a pencil that was long enough.

At night, when I would take a nap break between studies, some of the rowdies would come in and stick things down my cast--popcorn, peanuts, etc. When I would scratch, I would just push that stuff down farther, not knowing it was there.

One day my wrist started hurting. I hadn't bumped it, so didn't know what was wrong. It had been X-rayed weekly through the cast and supposedly, was healing all right. But it hurt. They took another picture and immediately removed my cast. They took out the top of a fountain pen, a handful of peanuts and popcorn, and a few paper clips, among other things.

They put on another cast, and I wore it into 1953, then a wrap for two months. I hoped I would never have to wear another cast again. As of this writing, I have been cast free. Although my luck had run out, it picked up again.

Tom And Pat's Wedding

It was summer and I was in school at OU, the last summer before starting my senior year. I didn't want to be in school, but I needed both the hours and some good grade points to graduate the following year. Mom had received a letter from the university stating I would not graduate with my class, and I was not about to let that happen.

Tom and Patricia Ashcraft were getting married that summer, on June 18 in San Diego, and I wanted to go. He had asked me to be his best man. I had to do some wheeling and dealing with professors to miss that much school, especially in the summer session. A 3-hour course in summer school met five days a week, and I was taking nine hours. I figured I needed at least four days plus a weekend to make the trip.

Tom was already there. He was still in the Naval Reserve, and had arranged for his two weeks of annual active duty to coincide with his wedding date. Or maybe they scheduled the wedding after he got his active duty dates. Anyway, it was a pretty slick operation.

I needed to be there. Not just because of being best man. Since Dad died five years earlier, Tom had been almost a father to me, even though he was away at Oklahoma A&M in college, and another two years in the Navy. In the previous year, Tom had finished his active duty obligation and went back to college, working on his masters degree. We were in the same fraternity at different schools, and that year, we really got to know one another as young adults. Tom became special to me after Dad died, in spite of all the problems we caused one another in previous years.

I was able to arrange it with my professors. The wedding was on a

Saturday, and I left on Tuesday or Wednesday on a Greyhound bus. The farthest I had ever been before was to Dallas--200 miles--the previous year to an OU-Texas football game. So I was excited about the trip. I got to Los Angeles and had to change buses for San Diego, and had my first encounter with the fruits and nuts of California. Innocent as I was, I managed to get to San Diego all right, where Tom met me. A sailor I had paled with on the bus kind of ran interference for me.

I have to admit I was somewhat reluctant to see Tom get married. He was important in my life--as a father figure, a brother, and friend. I thought all those things would be lost. And I was right--at least for the next few years. Mr. Ashcraft, Pat's father, had many of the same feelings. Here he was, losing his only daughter to an Okie who was taking her to corn country of Iowa to teach people how to farm.

We did, however, get them married. It was a fine wedding. The reception was in the Ashcraft's backyard, at midday on a hot Saturday. Mr. Ashcraft and I became buddies. We cried in our beer together over a bottle of I don't know what, mixed with something even stronger. It, combined with the heat, the sadness, and the excitement of the wedding hit me in a hurry, and bit me hard.

I never knew how he ended the day, and I don't remember too much about how mine ended--except sick. I had originally thought that my Mother and I would come back to Oklahoma together. Whether that was ever planned or not, I don't remember, but I know she canned the idea. She was so embarrassed about me that she wouldn't have gone anywhere with me. I would have rather waited a day or so, but I had to be back in class on Monday.

That afternoon, Frank Hall, Pat's brother, took me to the bus station, stopping once or twice along the freeway, and poured me onto the bus. Fortunately, the bus wasn't crowded, and I was able to take the entire back seat, which stretched all the way across. The other thing that was fortunate was that I didn't have to change buses. This was a direct flight with lots of landings and takeoffs in between.

After I settled in that seat, the next thing I remember was being awakened by a janitor in Oklahoma City. We were in the bus barn, and he was servicing the bus for its next trip. It was 2 a.m. Monday morning.

After several cups of coffee, I caught the next available bus to Norman, 20 miles away, and made my 7 o'clock class--and within a day, was back on schedule. I was not proud of myself. I apologized to Tom, Pat, her parents, and Mother several times. It took a while to get back in their good graces. I could rationalize, however, and say it was OK considering that I had lost a brother. I quickly got back into the swing of things, and finished the summer session with nine hours of A. That placed me on the Dean's honor roll, which got me some consideration when enrolling for the fall semester.

It was a distinct honor, or claim to fame, at the start of my senior year, to be the only one I knew, or heard of, who was on the Dean's honor roll and scholastic probation at the same time. I had gone through three years of college, barely making it by in the grade point department. Over that three years, I had done poorly in a couple of 5-credit hour science courses, and barely passed 10 hours of Latin. That kind of record will really bring the grade average down, no matter how good the rest of the grades are. I knew that when I went to summer school I had to graduate in 1956. I needed both the hours and grade points, especially the latter.

I took 34 hours my final two semesters, in spite of meeting and courting my fiancé and working full time. I finished both semesters with a 3.0+ grade average, which got me across the stage to receive a diploma.

At the end of the fall semester, I was still on the dean's honor roll and on scholastic probation. My overall grade average wasn't that bad, but once on the list, they keep you there awhile until they are sure you will make it. In the spring semester, I finally got off scholastic probation. Anything can be done if I wanted to do it bad enough. It was a real challenge, but I made it.

I Met Mary Kathryn

After completion of summer school, I was ready to start my senior year in college. I stayed in Norman and worked for an amusement park during the day, and for the Daily Oklahoman/Oklahoma City Times at night. I lived in a small room at the Newman Center, but had to move in the fall, as those rooms had been committed the previous spring. I could have lived at the fraternity house but didn't want to. I knew that I would be working almost full time, and that kind of social atmosphere no longer appealed to me. I would rather live outside the house, and take the parts of the social life I wanted.

There was a large influx of students that fall, more than the university could handle. I guess that was a boomer high school year, and there were many returning from Korea. This forced the University to relax its past policies regarding where students could live. The dorms were full.

As a result, many couples and singles living in big old houses opened up the second floor rooms to students. That's the kind of place I was looking for. I had been home for a few days, and borrowed a car to bring some stuff down and find a place to live. I only had three days to get moved in.

So, with a bunch of referrals from the student housing office, and the classified ads, I started looking. The first half dozen places I stopped at were full, and the next one had a room, which I didn't really care for. I decided to look some more, but kept that in my hip pocket.

Then, I stopped by the Goldie Twibell residence. Mrs. Twibell had three rooms upstairs--two singles and a double. There was a Greek, Kris (can't remember his last name) in one single and Chet Gorgas in the other. The double was half occupied by Bob Pearson, a senior who had lived in the same dorm with me when we were freshmen. I hadn't seen much of him since that first year.

The room was certainly nice enough. The location was just three blocks away from the campus, and the price was right. I just didn't know whether I wanted to live with Bob Pearson or not. As Mrs. Twibell and I walked back down the stairs, a beautiful girl, wearing a slip, appeared from a back room and walked through the living room.

"By the way," Mrs. Twibell said, "I want you to meet my granddaughter, Mary Kathryn, from Oklahoma City, who will also be living here this year--downstairs." Because of her attire, we were both embarrassed, but we did meet one another.

As I walked out onto the front porch, I decided that maybe Bob Pearson wasn't that bad, and I would be working at night in Oklahoma City, and probably wouldn't be around that much anyway. So, I took the room and took up residence three days later.

I didn't see Mary Kathryn much those first two weeks of school. We were going different ways on campus at different times. In fact, she spoke to me once at Campus Corner, and I didn't recognize her--the first time I saw her wearing glasses (and clothes). We finally had a coffee date on a class break, she came to a fraternity party, and pretty soon, we were holding hands. We hadn't dated long until I shortened her name to "Kathy" and I've called her that since. I was one of the few.

I thought I had lost the ballgame once when I shut a car door on her hand, but didn't. She was in extreme pain and her hand was bandaged for what seemed like weeks. I still didn't see much of her the first six weeks as Grandmother Twibell made her study at night --that's a Uuiversity philosophy--control the girls and you control the boys. I worked Thursday and Friday nights at the Daily Oklahoman, and Saturday, I always had work to do for someone covering OU football.

We didn't have much of a social life, but what we did have, we enjoyed. We were beginning to get real serious about one another. I took her home to meet Mom, who had sold the farm and now lived in Tulsa, and she took me home to meet her family. One of the common topics of conversation that semester on a double date or at a party was "Where do you live?" Our common response to that was "together," which often raised eyebrows. I know that it embarrassed her at times, as well as me. That's almost a standard reply today.

I decided I wanted to marry her. In early December, I went to Brochaus Jewelry, and signed away my life on a set of rings. I took her to the fraternity Christmas party. All of the guys' dates received a little stuffed puppy dog as a gift. I tied the engagement ring around its neck, then went through the trauma necessary to make sure she got the right one. As I recall, she didn't find the ring. I had to show her.

We were both extremely happy. I brought her back to Tulsa for part of the Christmas holidays, and we had a long talk with Mom. We wanted to get married right away, but Mom had the good sense of talking us into waiting until I graduated. There was no way I could support a wife with both of us in school, and Mom made it pretty clear that once married, we were on our own, for the most part. Mom told us the story of her wedding. The date was all set, and just a week before, Dad lost his job. Their wedding plans were put on the closet shelf for two years. So, we decided to wait. Her mother was happy about that too.

Being engaged caused other problems. Her mother and Grandmother Twibell were both uneasy about us being engaged, and living in the same house. (Haven't times changed?) One of us had to go. Grandmother Twibell needed the income from my rent, so it was Mary Kathryn who left. I think initially, she found a slot in a dorm--can't remember--but she dropped out of school second semester and returned home.

By that time, I was working full-time at night, Saturdays and some Sundays at the Oklahoma City Times. So, I got to see her a couple of times and on weekends. She started planning the wedding and we were married June 2, 1956, the day before I graduated. We had an apartment at NW 30th and Robinson in Oklahoma City. I went on active duty in August at Officer Candidate School Newport, RI. She joined me in November.

My Senior Year

My senior year in college was a big one. It was about finishing a degree program and getting that recognition; it was about getting into the profession of journalism as much as possible; it was about planning for a job, a future; it was about planning for a wedding; and it was about paying for all of that. It was a big year.

I finished my junior year as news editor, followed by sports editor of the Oklahoma Daily, OU student newspaper, and was ready for bigger things. The Daily Oklahoman/Oklahoma City Times, major morning and evening newspapers in central Oklahoma, had opened a news bureau on campus. Kuyk Logan, a graduate student, was a one man operator of the bureau and needed help. He had received approval to hire a student assistant and Louise Moore, faculty advisor for the Daily, had recommended me. It was my first real job as a news reporter. Kuyk and I covered the campus, each writing our own material and putting it on the teletype to the news room in Oklahoma City. Initially, he put his stamp of approval on all that I wrote but soon found that was not necessary. All that while carrying 16 credit hours. What a thrill it was to walk into our small office in the student union and hear the chat chat chat chat of the teletype. News items sent in the morning were picked up by the Times, and those in the afternoon picked up by the Daily Oklahoman.

From a contact, I got a job as stringer for International News Service, and got to cover the Oklahoma-Texas football game early in my senior year. What a thrill that was, sitting in the press box of the

Cotton Bowl, watching and recording that game, sitting right above that line that separated the Texas burnt orange and the Oklahoma red.

Ralph Sewell, City Editor of the Times, was so impressed with my work that he offered me a job on the city desk, starting second semester. More about that later. Meanwhile, I had a fiancé and a degree to pursue.

During my second and third year, I was part of a crew of students who covered high school football around the state for the Daily Oklahoman. The newspaper had the schedules of every school in the state and we covered every game in print in the Saturday paper. The big, local high school games were covered by the staff, lesser ones were covered by selected students and the rest by our crew by phone. The larger of these schools had stringers who would call in after the game with the results. For the rest, it was calling into the town, to the fire or police station, to a gas station, to the American Legion Hut, to whomever could tell you about the game. By midnight, we were on our way back to Norman, stopping at a local restaurant for a chicken leg and a beer. We continued this ritual during my senior year.

There was so much involvement - - working in the news bureau, working Friday nights in Oklahoma City on the sports desk, and dating Mary Kathryn, I don't know how I had time to go to school but I did. Sixteen hours a semester, all A's and B's.

Toward the end of the first semester, I had my first run-in with the law. Some of us were members of Sigma Delta Chi, professional journalism society, and we were encouraged to go to the national convention in Chicago. The convention would last about four days. It was a good opportunity to exchange ideas, hear renowned journalists speak, and to shop for jobs.

Four of us decided to go to the national convention. There were John Meek, George Gravely, Pierre-Rene North, and myself. We went to Chicago in John's car. He had a brother who had a used car dealership in central Oklahoma. If we would pick up three cars for him in the Chicago area and drive them back, he would help foot our bill. Sounded like a deal to us.

The final banquet/party ended about midnight on Saturday. We had arranged to pick up the cars south of Chicago at 2 a.m. Sunday.

That was all legitimate. What we didn't know was that in Illinois, when a car changes ownership, the license plates remain with the previous owner, not with the car. So, we had three cars with no tags at 2 a.m. Sunday and had to be in class Monday morning. We decided we couldn't wait until Monday to get tags. We hit the road. The only one legal was George Gravely, driving John's car.

We caravanned through southern Illinois and into Missouri. There were no interstates then--just Route 66. In central and southern Missouri, it was hilly, the road was laced with curves, and it was only two lanes. The lead driver--who changed frequently--would go over the top of a hill or around a curve, see that the road was clear, and wave the others to come on around slower traffic. We wanted to get back.

A State Trooper stopped us in the hill country of Missouri. It was real country. He cited all four of us for speeding, passing on hills, and passing on curves; and the three of us for driving with no plates, which was the real killer.

The trooper's first thought was that the cars were stolen. He took us to the closest county jail, which was deep in the sticks, and locked us up. There was no hope for getting out until we faced the judge, who had gone fishing and would not be back until Tuesday. The jail was a dingy place--dirt floors, and only a cot and a pot. The only lighting came through the bars on the window.

Somehow, late that afternoon--we had been there four or five hours -- a bail arrangement was made through John's brother, and we were released. We came back to Norman in John's car, the other three being impounded. John's brother paid all the fines and had to send three drivers to Missouri to bring the cars back. He didn't make much off that deal.

We got back in school Tuesday, and bore the brunt of a lot of kidding. In spite of everything, it was a good trip. It was during that trip that John Meek and I became good friends.

I don't know what happened to Pierre, or where he went with his career. For awhile after graduation, George worked for the Times with me, then on the sports desk of the Tulsa World. Then, I lost track of him. In later years, I would connect with him again. John Meek was the big success.

John got involved in politics. He was in the press organization of Oklahoma senator Robert Kerr and later worked for both Senators Bobby Kennedy and Lyndon Johnson. He then became a successful lobbyist in Washington, D.C. In later years, when I was stationed in Washington, D.C., we saw John several times. He invited us to a party one night and introduced us to a fledgling young guitar player named John Denver, who was singing with the Chad Mitchell Trio. We got to see John sing several times that year. Had it not been for that time in jail, I most likely would never have met him. It has always been said that out of every "bad" comes something "good."

At the start of the second semester, my work in the bureau had been recognized and Ralph Sewell, City editor, offered me a job on the City Desk of the Times. I would be writing material for an area section published weekly for the northwest part of the city. I accepted. I had my own press card and could use a staff car to chase down stories. All of my classes were in the morning so I would catch a bus after noon, work through the evening then catch the last bus back at midnight. On Saturdays, I would come in early and work on the city desk, writing primarily obituaries. Saturday afternoons and Sundays were catch-up on my schooling.

All that, plus courting, plus following OU football added up to a big semester. On top of that, Mary Kathryn and I wanted to get married, but Mom had talked us into waiting.

So, we married at the end of school, one day before graduation ceremonies.

Lonnie Pence, my Tribune Boss
and me, 1952

H.S. Graduation Picture

Last of the "all night parties," before we
all go our separate ways. This one at our
house in about 1953.

Newt and Maggie at The Club

Graduation from OU

A Visit to Mike's on
my way to OCS, 1956

The Day I Became Jack

A ll my life, up to my senior year in college, I had been known by my first name of John. Looking back into family ancestry, I could find brothers' and sister's names, including middle names. There was a grand-relative somewhere who carried the name. However, there was not a John David anywhere in the family lineage. My oldest brother Horace had been successful in changing his name to Mike. Michael had been the name he accepted at confirmation. I had envied him, and always wanted to change my name, but I didn't know the name I wanted. So, after three years of college, I was still John.

My new career on the Oklahoma City Times changed all that and gave me the opportunity for a new name. The career was almost short lived. On any assignment, we could take a staff car, which always impressed me. I even had an amber flashing light which, kept in the seat, could be plugged into the cigarette lighter and put on top of the car. WOW. There was a newspaper policy that said if we got any traffic tickets (non-moving violations), we could turn them in with the car, and the newspaper took care of them.

I misunderstood the policy, or didn't read it, or whatever, but I thought it applied to all tickets. One night, I was between stories on the northwest side, in a rush, backed out of a driveway and drove the wrong way for a half-block on a boulevard street to get to an intersection. It was faster.

There was a police car at the corner and my staff car and press card didn't impress the officer a bit. I got two tickets--speeding, and going the wrong way. I didn't notice that the tickets had a court appearance date. In fact, I didn't pay any attention to them. When I got back to the office, I left them in the car with a parking ticket I had gotten earlier in the day.

The sports editor for the Oklahoman was John Cronley, who, because of time there, was a figurehead at the Oklahoman. He was a real fixture. I had gotten to know him through my previous experience of working high school football, and had learned to stay well clear of his path. John had been on vacation when I got the tickets, and came back two weeks later. By that time, my court appearance date had come and gone, and I didn't appear.

He had been back about two days when a warrant was issued for my arrest and the police came to get me. I was still rather new, and my name wasn't exactly a household word, and the rather new receptionist said to the officers, "John Connery? You must mean John Cronley." To her, that was close enough.

The police went to John Cronley's office to arrest him. He wasn't a bit pleased about it. When he got it straightened out, he was fuming. I think the sportswriters around him kidded him about it. "Whoever was responsible," he raved that he would have their job. My boss, Ralph Sewell, went to bat for me and I was saved, although my probationary period was extended. I was told, however, that I would have to change my name. The best I could come up with was Jack. That seemed to satisfy everyone, so Jack I became--at least at the Times. I was still John at OU, and with my family. But I liked Jack better, so over the next year, it slowly changed.

Except for my brother Mike, who had changed his name from Horace, and had sympathy for me, my family still called me John. So did all my high school classmates, who came back for our class reunions in later years.

Oh well, call me anything you want--just don't call me late for dinner.

So You Want To Be An Officer?

A t home over Easter of my senior year in 1956, I ran into the head of the local draft board, an old family friend. "You graduate this spring, don't you?"

"Yes sir." I replied. "Then, I'll start on my career to be a great sportswriter."

"You're gonna have to put that off," he said. "Your deferment runs out and we're gonna draft you into military service. Sportswriting will have to wait a few years."

We spent the next week checking this out and found it to be true. I remembered the stories my Dad told and decided I did not want to be a foot soldier. Then, when back at OU, I came across a naval officer recruiting team in the student union one day. I couldn't wait to complete the paperwork and the next week, I was on my way to Dallas for more testing and a physical exam. Maybe I could be a naval officer, like my brothers Mike and Tom.

It took a while, mostly because of physical considerations; two trips to Dallas, and finally a couple of phone calls to Washington, but I finally met all the requirements for selection to Naval Officer Candidate School. I started the application process in March of 1956, and was selected in July. Because of the two phone calls to Washington, I got the red carpet treatment my second trip to Dallas, and was selected. I was then scheduled to enter training at Newport, R.I., for 17 weeks starting in mid August.

When I left that August, Mary Kathryn was already pregnant, so I felt I had to make it. I travelled to Newport RI with Dave Mann, a guy

I had met in Oklahoma City who was also going. We did a weekend in New York City, then went to Newport to go to work.

That 17 weeks was grueling, but not like the movie "An Officer and a Gentleman." The emphasis was 95 percent on academics rather than the physical aspects. The only similarities were the girls. They were there: we called them the "Fall River Debs," from the textile mills of Fall River, Mass. We carried a load of six subjects, ranging from Marine Engineering to Weapons to Celestial Navigation with three others interspersed.

I was never much of a good student. I always had a hard time reading and remembering. If, however, I could get my hands on it, I could learn it. The course material was so different than anything I had taken in four years of college, which made things even more difficult.

We had a series of aptitude tests the first week, along with complete physical examinations, lots of shots, fitting for uniforms, haircuts, finding our way around the compound--no one would ever call it a campus--and all that other indoctrination stuff.

I was assigned to a counselor, a chief petty officer, who reviewed my test results, and he flat told me I would never make it. He suggested that I consider getting out of OCS now, saving me a tough time and the Navy a lot of money. I thought about it that night, and gave serious consideration to that option. In two years, I could be back at the Oklahoma City Times. Then, I thought about my pregnant wife, and how different life as an enlisted man, a seaman apprentice, would be, compared to that of an officer. The only advantage would be that I would be out of the Navy sooner.

I decided that the counselor didn't know what he was talking about, and that I would make it. I had to. Officer candidates with low grades go before a review board every four weeks. I never had to do that, but I was real close a couple of times.

I got through the first four weeks all right then we got into celestial navigation and the operation of weapons systems. I soon found that the six subjects were just too much for me to handle the study requirements effectively each week and keep good grades across the board. I felt sure I would flounder if I tried to keep up with all of them, so I devised a system. I identified the three subjects I absolutely had to hit hard each week, then with the remaining three, picked two to study each week, alternating every week.

On the one I dropped each week, I didn't open a book--just tried to remember as much as possible from class lectures. Occasionally, I would "tree" (have a weekly failing grade) the course I neglected, but never two, which would get me restricted and on the way to the review board. The next week, I would bring that grade up and fall off in another.

One of my three roommates was a psychologist with a masters degree--a really brilliant person. He didn't study--but instead would sit there all evening trying to psychoanalyze himself to figure why he wasn't making it. I knew why--and told him several times--he just wasn't studying. We came back to the barracks one afternoon and he was gone. The review board had washed him out.

There was another guy in our section who washed out. He was carrying a 3.2 grade average--much better than mine--but his aptitude tests indicated he should be making a 3.6 or 3.7. The review board thought he was loafing, and the Navy did not want loafers.

We saw several go that way--some of whom had become good friends. They would just disappear, and we wouldn't see them again. They were tough to lose. It always made me wonder, "When will it be my turn?"

Mary Kathryn came about Thanksgiving and stayed the rest of the time. We found her a room in a home converted to a rooming house. As long as we kept our grades up, we would get liberty after personnel inspection, about noon on Saturday until midnight Sunday. Watching her get bigger and bigger, and knowing how poor we were on seaman's pay were real incentives to get through the program. There was a program where marginal students could "roll back" into the class behind and finish with them. We had a couple in our section from the previous class. I thought about that, but wasn't interested in spending that additional time in a Newport winter.

Then one day, they got the 800 (we started with almost 1,100) of us who were still there assembled in the gym, standing at attention in formation. They gave us the oath, and said, "Gentlemen, be seated." We were officers. We had made it.

There is an old custom in the Navy (probably in all services) that the first enlisted man who salutes a newly commissioned officer gets paid a dollar. That honor is traditionally reserved for the company chief. He got my dollar, but I wanted someone else to get a dollar too. I found that counselor who, it seemed like years ago, said I wouldn't make it, and stood him at attention. He smiled, saluted and offered congratulations, and I stuck a dollar in his hand. It was well worth it.

We left Newport that day, on our way to Tulsa and Oklahoma City for Christmas. Then, it would be on to Key West, Fla., in early January for a five week school. To get into the traffic pattern to head west, we had to take a ferry across Narragansett Bay. I stood on the deck of that ferry, taking in the cold salt air, watching the gulls, watching ships as they entered and left the bay, and watching the shoreline disappear behind us; not realizing how much I would learn to enjoy that scene; not realizing how much that salt air would get into my blood; and not realizing that this would be my profession for the next 21 years.

I had great hopes for the future--hopes for me, my wife, and my family (soon to be). Those hopes, at the time, lay not in a career as a naval officer, but as a writer. This was my dream and I would come back to the Oklahoma City Times and start fulfilling it. The next three years would only be carrying out an obligation to my country. Then, I could get on with my life (our lives). Little did I know how different a course our lives would take over the next few years. But I was ready to take it on.

Influences

When one gets to be my age, he occasionally looks back and thinks about the things and people who shaped his life to be what it is. I've thought a lot about this during the writing of this book, and I believe it is a very important part of this book. The "things" are not my concern. People are what this is about.

It has not been difficult to identify four people, outside of my family, who had a great influence on my life. It would be difficult, in some cases, to tell you just what that influence was, and the effect it had on shaping my life. In some cases, I don't even know. Perhaps a lot of it is role modeling, although I don't think so. If not, then what? All I know is that I sense that each of them, in their own way, had a profound effect on what I became--what I am good or bad.

After identifying these four, I searched back through my memory to see if there was someone else. No one can touch them. This is about them--my relationship with them, and where possible, some kind of a hint as to what that influence was. This is written not only to be a major part of this book; not only to be of possible interest to the reader; but also to be a tribute to them. At this writing, three are deceased, so it is a tribute to their memory.

Psychologists say that an individual is "shaped" by the age of six. I do not believe this. The first one of these people came into my life at the age of 11, and I met the last one when I was 22. Although these people perhaps had only influence on the direction of my life, certainly that direction involved shaping, or reshaping. It has been interesting, looking back on life and identifying the people who shaped my life.

Fred Gesin

I met Fred Gesin when I was in the sixth or seventh grade. He was the new high school band director. Perhaps he had been there the year before, but I don't think so. I said, "Mr. Gesin, I want to be in the band."

"First of all," he replied, "My name is Gesin. Call me that." Secondly, he asked what I wanted to play.

That response set the tone for our relationship over the next six years--not only mine with him, but his relationship with anyone else who came in contact with "Gesin." My parents had taught me better--respect adults and address them accordingly, and always say "sir" or "maam." But with Gesin, it was different. However, the salutation, "Hey Gesin," was always said with respect.

In those days, no student, at least publicly, wanted to be too close to a teacher. The tag "teacher's pet" would catch up with you. I'm sure that this is true in a lot of school communities today. No one wants to get too close to a teacher. Although Gesin was a teacher of music, that didn't apply to him. Making that adjustment, along with learning to holler "Gesin" was difficult for me, but he went a long way to make it easier.

"Gesin" was his name, and "music was the name of the game." Those last words are mine, not his. Years later, I watched the movie"Music Man," and couldn't help but feel that Professor Harold Hill and Gesin were a lot alike, and perhaps had gone to school together. The big difference was that Harold Hill was a con man. Gesin wasn't. Gesin was a producer. When his band marched out, it was a Gesin production, and he was never surprised about the quality he saw.

"I want to play the drums," I said at that first encounter. "My brother played drums, ya know, and I want to be better than he was." From that, the relationship started. A couple of years earlier, I had played the "sticks" in a rhythm band and I thought I was pretty good at creating and maintaining rhythm.

The next year, after beginners' band, I was playing in the high school concert band, and the year following, the marching band. I suppose it took longer for the latter because I had to grow enough to march with a drum.

Over the next six years, Gesin became a way of life. Any free time at school was usually spent in the band room. Gesin liked to tell stories, especially about fishing. He told others, like the one about the two country brothers who made a six-shooter. His office was just inside the band room door, a converted army barracks which served Broken Arrow High for at least 15 years.

Walk in there any time of the day when he wasn't directing or teaching, and he had a captive audience--telling stories. He had a way of educating kids with stories. He was never too busy to listen to a problem. He was a tremendous help to me after Dad died.

He was one anyone my age would look up to, and most everyone did, whether in band or not. He could be stern when required, but he never used his position of teacher as a lever to get you to do what he wanted, or what you were suppose to do. He didn't have to. It just happened.

I remember the time when we (the new crop coming into band the year I did) first got uniforms. There was very little money in the school budget for band uniforms. I think the school bought them from the Salvation Army--or from another school which had bought from the Salvation Army and used them a year or two. He tossed me a coat and trousers and said, like he did to everyone else, "Take them home and have your mother make them fit."

We were such a ragtag looking outfit. But we could play. Years later, I came back to watch the Rooster Day parade and watched the current edition of the BA band march down the street. How fine they looked. How sharp they were dressed. It brought a tear to my eye when I thought about how we looked. I voiced that to an old timer next to me and he said, "They really look good, but they only know one song." We could play anything, and did, and it was Gesin who made it possible. That band today has won all sorts of state and national awards, has appeared in the Rose Bowl parade and I think one presidential inauguration parade. It all started with Fred Gesin 70 years ago.

Gesin played the trumpet. And he did it well. I well remember our fight song at BA. Gesin brought in another, which came to mean almost as much. He would start our drums with a brisk 4/4 beat, and after about 16 bars, would step out in front of the band, cock that trumpet, and play "Marie." That always brought the crowd to its feet. After about 16 bars of that, the band would join in. I don't know the reason for "Marie," where it came from, or what made it special to him, but they still talk about it in Broken Arrow today, years later. "Marie" may have won as many games as Ragsdale's coaching. His rendition of Taps at Baccalaureate, or his Auld Lang Syne at Commencement always brought tears to many eyes.

We had two big celebrations a year in Broken Arrow. Rooster Day in the spring, and Cotton Jubilee in the fall. The Chamber of Commerce, two or three days before each, would sponsor a booster trip to surrounding communities to promote it. We would always take a pep band. That's covered earlier in another story. I do remember one we made in the Spring in the rain. Off at 8 a.m., visit 6-8 towns plus a live radio broadcast at noon in Tulsa, and get back at 6 p.m., soaked, drums wet, lips blown out, and we had concert band practice at 8 p.m. The Regional Band concert finals were the next day in Tahlequah. Gesin told us how good we were in spite of the colds already starting to develop.

He said we were good--and we believed him. He was right. We got a first place in regional competition.

One day, at practice, Dean Hess, a senior drummer (I was a junior), and I were scrapping a little bit to see who got to stand in front of the music stand. I really don't know why because neither of us read music that well. We kept pushing and shoving, until it got disruptive to practice. Gesin warned us--but it didn't stop. Finally, he waded through clarinets, French horns, trombones and trumpets to get to us. He had reached his "end." He picked both of us up by the collar, one in each hand, and banged us together. Drums flew everywhere. Then he opened the back door and pushed us out. He didn't have to say a word.

When I was a sophomore, I was a key member of the football marching band, because the lead drummer was drum major. I was also playing football, but had not made the traveling squad. One Thursday, about halfway through the season, because of a couple of injuries, and the fact that I had had a good practice week, my name came up on the traveling squad. Nobody, especially Gesin and me, expected that. I was ecstatic. I had made the team. Gesin said he didn't think he could release me from the marching band. I was devastated. The coach had said there was little chance I would play--but still I had made the team. Gesin said he would think about it that night and let me know Friday morning. I didn't sleep much that night. The next morning, Gesin smiled, and said "Go." I didn't say a word. I didn't have to. Gesin just realized how much it meant to me. And I did get to play. I had marched with the band at a football game for the last time.

Bus trips with the band were fun, especially to a Saturday parade. Gesin not only directed the band, but he drove the bus. Sarah, his wife, who had no connection with the school, often went with us; especially when we went to Tulsa. She would shop while we would march, and was always late getting back to the bus. Gesin often wanted to leave her, but we wouldn't let him.

When I was graduating, and planning to go to OU, Gesin arranged an audition for me with the Director of the OU marching band. What a thrill that was. I made it. That is also covered earlier. In the summer, Gesin taught clinics, played in dance bands, and also played in a twilight concert series sponsored by the Tulsa Parks Department. A group of Union musicians put together various types of concerts during the summer--jazz, concert, march music, etc. Many of us would go together, and all go down to see him at intermission. That was a thrill--knowing someone in the orchestra.

Fred also taught driver education. He taught us to drive and he told fish stories there too. When I came home to my Mother's funeral in 1969, I had a long visit with Gesin. He was no longer band director, but was a high school counselor. They couldn't have picked a better choice. We talked a lot about old times, concerts, football games, booster trips, and fishing.

The next time I came back in 1971, I found that Gesin had died. About 1978, after we had moved back to Oklahoma, I located Sarah, his wife, and we had lunch together a couple of times. It's really great to look back on the kind of relationship we all had with Gesin. As I have written this, I had to wipe away a tear or two.

Willie Kennedy

Willie Kennedy was my sophomore and junior English teacher.

Willie was a large woman--not overweight--just large. It seems that I've written these words before, and now that I think of it, she kind of fits the same description of my Aunt Maggie, described earlier, as Hostess of The Club. Willie had a good sense of humor, liked to laugh, and she was a real pleasure to have as a teacher.

Willie was married to Perry, a junior high teacher who also coached junior high basketball. Perry was kind of a Clark Kent looking guy, and I had to feel sorry for him, being so mild and meek, and being married to the aggressive, outgoing Willie, who was, or at least seemed to be, bigger than he was. I felt sorry for him--until I saw him on the basketball court--coaching kids. After that, there was no question in my mind about who was boss in his family. However, she may have been a year or two older than Perry.

Willie taught English, and more than that, she taught character. She taught attitude, she taught responsibility, and those things I always enjoyed learning from her. I would leave class looking forward to doing the homework assigned. She instilled that kind of thinking.

In my senior year, I decided I wanted to major in journalism. We had a journalism class that year, and I enrolled in it because Glenn Cone did. Willie taught me the importance of the written word. She helped me make my career education decision. If I'da only stuck with that decision, and got out of the Navy, I believe I could have been an excellent columnist. Willie made me believe I could.

Willie was another teacher, who, like Gesin, you could get close to without being a "teacher's pet." I remember a time when school was closed because of snow, and Keith Boyce and I decided to go rabbit hunting. He came to my house with his shotgun, and we started out. Willie and Perry were among the few non-American Airlines people who lived in the addition next to us. We decided to stop and make sure Willie and Perry were all right. After an hour of doughnuts and coffee, and good conversation, Keith and I decided they were okay, and we went on our hunting expedition. We had wanted Perry to go with us, but their dog was missing and Perry remained home to look for him.

In my junior year literature class, she had the confrontation with Shelby Smith about fixing a tractor vs. studying Shelly and Keats. In the spring of that year, it was Willie who blew the whistle on me about the junior-senior fight, which resulted in my being suspended for three weeks. This is covered earlier. I was angry with her about it, but she was doing her job as she saw it.

In our junior English class (Literature), Willie gave me something. She did not realize it but it was a true gift. To her, it was an assignment. We had to memorize and be prepared to recite the last eight lines of the poem, *Thanatopsis*, by William C. Bryant. *Thanatopsis* is Greek, and translated, means a "view of death. I memorized it, recited it, and I got an A. But what is more important is that it has always been with me. Those eight lines were on the bulkhead of my shipboard stateroom in the Suez crisis and the Bay of Pigs; on another ship during two deployments to Vietnam; and otherwise in the back of my mind. I have no idea about what the lines before them said--I didn't have to learn them, but these eight lines have always been especially important to me, and are worthy of being repeated here:

THANATOPSIS

By William C. Bryant
(The Last Eight Lines)
So live, that when thy summons comes to join
The innumerable caravan, which moves to that mysterious realm,
Where each shall take his chamber
In the silent halls of death,
Thou go not, like the quarry slave at night, scourged to his dungeon, but
sustained and soothed by an unfaltering trust,
Approach thy grave like one
Who wraps the drapery of his couch
About him and lies down to pleasant dreams.

Years later, I visited Willie Kennedy. We wanted her to come to a class reunion, but she was too ill. She was in her 70s and had bone cancer. She was sharp as a tack, and remembered everything we talked about, and even corrected me on some points.

Louise Beard Moore

Louise Beard Moore (LBM, she always initialed on her notes) was faculty advisor of the Oklahoma Daily, school newspaper at the University of Oklahoma. If she had faculty status, it most likely was as an instructor. She was a seasoned newspaperwoman who was there to teach and shepherd fledgling young journalists. In addition to being faculty advisor, she taught some lab courses in writing, editing and layout.

As Willie Kennedy taught me the importance of the written word, LBM taught me the importance of the truthfulness of the written word. Eliminate bias, prejudice, personal feelings, etc., from your thinking in reporting news. Read the newspapers today and you will find a lot of prominent writers who never took that course.

Louise never believed in quoting an unnamed source--unless it was obviously for a good reason. Any major breaking news article today has so many undisclosed sources quoted that it is almost phony. That was not LBM. And I think she was right.

Louise was seasoned. She had seen both the bad and good in news reporting, and had probably experienced them both. She never rattled. She sponsored a paper that was published daily to a community of 20,000 people. The Daily was just as subject to criticism, suits, etc., as any newspaper is. She had another cross to bear, however. That was the policy line of the University of Oklahoma, the publisher. She would never kowtow to it. Freedom of the press was of the utmost importance to her.

She was always calm, collected, and never raised her voice, never stomped her foot and said, "No" to what we wanted to do with the newspaper. She only offered calm, logical advice based on her experience, and we most often followed it; sometimes didn't, and I'm sure she often went to bed at night wondering whether her livelihood would be there tomorrow, or who would sue her, the University, or the editor, etc., about what.

When I was news editor, and occasionally when I was sports editor, she would come to me and say, "Do you really want to do it this way?" or "Is this what you really mean?" There was never any of the "You can't do it,"--just the opportunity to sit back and think it through again. Sometimes we would go along with her--sometimes not. It was our paper and she fully supported us.

When you screwed up, she could be harsh. Her words, although always quiet, could have a deep cutting effect, and you knew you were wrong.

In my early days on the staff of the paper (junior year), I saw her go through a megabucks libel suit because of misplacement of a comma in a news story, which put an entirely different meaning on a sentence. She never wavered, and fully supported the editor. She always stood tall, and she never let down on any of us by telling us what a pain we were to her happy living. That was newspapering in its finest form.

Tom Murphy

I was 22 when I met Tom Murphy. One would think that by that age, lifelong goals would be decided. I thought they were, but as I learned, they weren't.

I was a brand new ensign in the Navy, and I went to Long Beach, California, with a pregnant wife, and I reported to the U.S.S. Reaper (MSO 467). Lieutenant Tom Murphy was my first commanding officer. It was early February 1957 when I reported. We had found a small apartment on the beach. Mary Kathryn was pregnant, and could deliver any time within the next two weeks.

The Reaper was in the shipyard, just finishing up an overhaul. I was so wet behind the ears, I didn't know which end of the ship to salute when I went aboard.

I was escorted immediately to the executive officer's stateroom, and met Lt. George Sutcliffe. George was a late WWII and Korean vintage Merchant Marine Officer who came back in the Navy to finish his career. He had one eye that never opened or closed fully. He had the appearance of being mean, and it was not a facade. George scared the hell out of this new ensign. I soon learned that the officer I was to relieve was already gone, and George had to take over his duties in the interim, and gone on the in-port watch bill, awaiting my arrival. Needless to say, he was glad to see me, but I couldn't tell. In later weeks, George would holler, "Hey Boot, you better listen. One day I'll be gone and you'll have to do it by yourself."

George took me up to meet THE COMMANDING OFFICER, Lt. Tom Murphy. Tom had been selected for lieutenant commander, but his number had not come up yet to put on the third stripe. George Sutcliffe, as frightening as he was, was a teddy bear compared to my first encounter with Tom Murphy.

Tom was big. About 6'5"--had to stoop in some places to walk through his cabin - - and weighed about 230. My initial thought was that if he had been playing for the University of Oklahoma, we could have won the national championship in 1955.

Tom was ugly. His head was about a size bigger than his 230 pound frame. He had kind of a snaggle tooth in front. When I sat down, I was shaking in my boots with real fear. My first impression was that this man should have been in Al Capone type movies instead of the U.S. Navy, much less have command of a ship.

First question: "I understand you are from the University of Oklahoma."

Answer: "Yes Sir."

Second Question: "I understand that you just completed Officer Candidate School."

Answer: "Yes Sir."

"Well, Mister Connery, you have noticed that the officer you are to relieve is no longer here. He was a graduate of the University of Oklahoma, and was commissioned out of OCS. I fired him two weeks ago. Mister Connery, as you can see, you have two strikes against you already."

That ended the interview. Here I was--in a brand new environment, a brand new profession, in a different geographic area, with a pregnant wife and two strikes against me already. Talk about being scared. I was.

He got my attention. I soon learned, however, that Tom Murphy was a jewel to work for. He would give out all the responsibility one could handle--and more--and the authority to carry it out. Then, he would back you up fully. And if in carrying that out, you screwed up, requiring a session in the woodshed, that would be there, too.

Tom Murphy was a firm believer in teaching junior officers (there were three of us) to handle the ship in every evolution it was supposed to do. That includes leaving the pier, doing the job at sea, and returning to the pier.

After a short while, I had no problem getting the ship underway, or doing the job; but getting back alongside the pier was a real nightmare. I almost rammed the pier once, got the anchor hung up in a pier light post once, and almost put us on the rocks a third time.

Each time, Tom had to take over at the point of "extremis" and correct for my mistakes. He always waited until the last minute to do this. Tom sensed that I was losing confidence in myself. He didn't know that I didn't have that much to lose.

On the fourth time, when I was approaching the pier, although everything was going OK, I kept looking back over my shoulder waiting for him to take over. He sensed that, and I looked back one time, and he wasn't there. I looked down over the bridge to the forecastle, and he was down there talking to the Boatswain. I had no choice. I had to do it.

He had put his career and his ship in my hands, without being close enough to counteract anything I did wrong. It was a clumsy mooring, but with no damage, and I did it. He made my day, and I went on to be an outstanding shiphandler, until the day some 13 years later, when I let complacency take charge and had an accident handling a ship.

Tom gave each of us a letter, authorizing us to take the ship to sea in any emergency without his presence. He had that much confidence in us. What that letter did we thought, was keep somebody else from coming aboard and taking over in that situation, should it occur. That's confidence. It did so much for us. It almost happened once. The Fleet Commander would initiate an exercise to see how fast ships could get underway and deploy to a pre-designated latitude and longitude. When the word came, usually about 0500, the Officer of the Deck had to act. We didn't have any phones on the ship, just a pay phone at the head of the pier, and we always had a roll of dimes to activate a recall.

One such morning, Tom almost didn't make it back at the time of sailing. He got hung up in traffic at the Terminal Island drawbridge. I was getting the ship underway, as he came running down the pier. I was able to hold the bow in to the pier while a seaman helped him climb aboard through the lifelines. I often wished I would have ignored him and gone to sea without him. I don't think he would have worried.

My wife and I grew to love Tom, and his wife, Gay, dearly. They were always special to us. Tom and Gay were proxy godparents to my first child, Kathleen. When she was severely burned six months later, they were with us every day.

Tom was wronged by the Navy System. As CO of the Reaper, he was in his third shipboard command as a lieutenant. He was up and coming. The Navy had sent him to PG school and he had a masters in nuclear physics. Tom got crossways with a division commander, before my time, and his career was ruined. He never made Commander, and retired on 20 years. He was a victim of a good system that does not admit it occasionally makes a mistake.

I last saw Tom and Gay in 1964 when we were both stationed in Norfolk, Va. We had lunch together a number of times, and they were always good visits. After he retired, he joined the faculty of a university in Connecticut, teaching physics.

One of the hardest things I had to do in the Navy was tell Tom I had been promoted to commander. I was in the Med when I put the stripes on, so it was five months later when we came back that I could call him. It was awfully tough to do, knowing that I had achieved something he had not--but should have.

Why is this man coming along in my life when I am 22, married, and soon to be a father, one of these four people who had so much influence on my life? If my second or third CO had been my first, I would have gotten out of the Navy in three years, and would have become a writer. But I had Tom Murphy, who was a prince of a man, as my first commanding officer. Through his demeanor, his personality, his leadership, and a whole bunch of other characteristics, he convinced me, without outwardly trying, that if the Navy was good enough for him as a career, it was certainly good enough for me.

What did these four people teach me? Why are they the ones singled out as being the more important influences in my life? I guess it boils down to truth, honesty, pride, responsibility and confidence, among other things.

-30-

Printed in the United States
By Bookmasters